AN
AMISH
ADVENTURE

AN AMISH ADVENTURE

A Workbook for Color in Quilts

Second Edition

Roberta Horton

C&T PUBLISHING

*To the Amish Quiltmakers—
thanks for the inspiration.*

Copyright © 1996 by Roberta Horton.
Cover:
Shades of Amish
Roberta Horton
Berkeley, CA
Pieced by George Taylor and Roberta Horton
Quilted by Roberta Horton

Photography by Lynn Kellner and Sharon Risedorph,
Kellner/Risedorph Photography San Francisco, CA

Design by Bonnie Jean Smetts

Published by C&T Publishing
P.O. Box 1456
Lafayette, CA 94549

ISBN: 0-914881-01-9 (First Edition)
0-57120-005-3 (Second Edition)

Horton, Roberta.
    An Amish adventure: a workbook for color in quilts / Roberta Horton. — 2nd ed.
        p.   cm.
    Includes bibliographical references.
    ISBN 1-57120-005-3 (pbk.)
    1. Patchwork—United States—Design. 2. Quilts. Amish.
I. Title.
TT835.H6 1996
746.9'7—dc20   95-45003
                                                            CIP

Crayola is a registered trademark of Binney & Smith, Inc.

Printed in Hong Kong

10 9 8 7 6 5 4 3 2 1

CONTENTS

✦

FOREWORD

I met my first Amish quilt more than 20 years ago. I had heard about Amish quilts, but didn't know what they looked like or what made them special. As soon as I saw that Diamond at the quilt show, I knew it was unique.

I have been fascinated with Amish quilts ever since. You may wonder where a Californian finds Amish quilts to study. Quilters living in the San Francisco Bay Area during the 1970s and 1980s had a unique opportunity: The Esprit de Corp headquarters, located in a warehouse district of San Francisco, housed a fantastic quilt collection. Then-owner Doug Tompkins refined his collection over the years so that it was all Amish. He generously allowed quilters to view this collection, and thus be inspired. For this I thank him. Many other local collectors and quilt stores have been just as generous in sharing their Amish quilts through quilt shows.

I had always dreamed of going to Lancaster County, Pennsylvania, to see the Amish in person. This dream came true in 1980. Upon my return, I immediately began to teach a six-week Amish series of quilting classes. I learn through my teaching, and was amazed how much could be learned about color from these quilts. My goal was to emulate, rather than copy. According to *Webster's New World Dictionary*, emulate means "to try to equal or surpass, or to rival successfully."

After the six-week class, my students seemed confident in their use of color and in bordering. They kept requesting to go further, so a second six-week class was added. This is represented by Lessons 7 through 10.

I have since visited Amish areas in other parts of Pennsylvania, as well as in Indiana, Ohio, Iowa, Oklahoma and Canada. I continue to read everything I find about the Amish and to attend any lecture on the subject. I have traveled thousands of miles to attend quilt shows featuring Amish quilts. This love affair doesn't end. I have also been fortunate to share this fascination with other quilters in Japan, New Zealand, South Africa and in Europe.

Many of the statements made in this book are based on my thoughts as a quilter, rather than as a historian or an artist. One quilter to another. I hope that you enjoy the conversation and will join in....

INTRODUCTION

✚

Quilts are a reflection of the people who make them and the time period in which they are made. To understand and better appreciate Amish quilts, then, you need some knowledge of who the Amish are.

The story begins in Switzerland, where in 1525 a group called the Brethren separated from the state church. They eventually became known as Mennonites, after Menno Simons, one of their early leaders. The Mennonites believed in separation of church and state, saying that man couldn't swear an oath of allegiance to anyone but God. They also espoused adult rather than infant baptism, since a child didn't know enough about true faith to make a commitment. The state church banned the new religion and a long, bloody history commenced. Many Mennonites were tortured and killed, and even when this was finally outlawed, they were still considered second-class citizens, unable to own land and forced to pay double taxes for the right to be different. This pattern was repeated in each new central European country into which they migrated.

In 1693, Jacob Ammann, a Mennonite elder, formed his own splinter group. He felt that the Mennonites were too worldly. He also wanted to instigate the practice of shunning, whereby transgressors were ostracized. The Amish, as they

became known, also had a difficult time in Europe and eventually migrated to America, seeking religious freedom. They now live in twenty-two states and in Ontario, Canada. About seventy percent of the 140,000 Amish (including children) live in Ohio, Pennsylvania, and Indiana. In addition, there are or have been communities in Arkansas, Delaware, Florida, Illinois, Iowa, Kansas, Kentucky, Maryland, Michigan, Minnesota, Missouri, Nebraska, New Mexico, New York, Oklahoma, Oregon, Tennessee, Virginia, and Wisconsin. About three-fourths of these communities came into being after 1940.

The Amish live in rural farming communities. They belong to church districts of from fifteen to forty families, usually with no more than seventy five adult members. Many similarities exist between the various districts, but also many differences. The Amish rules of order, called the *Ordnung*, are oral rather than written, allowing for many interpretations and therefore much flexibility. The bishop and elders of a district make the decisions on interpretation.

The Amish speak three languages. High German is used for their Bible and three-hour church services. Among each other they speak Pennsylvania Dutch, which is really a German dialect with some English words thrown in. They also communicate with the non-Amish world in English, and therefore call outsiders "English."

Their clothes set them apart from the outside world. Again, within the entire group there is much variation but within a church district or area, there is the feeling of a uniform. Though not considered a uniform by the Amish, it serves the same purpose: identifying the group to both its members and outsiders. In other words, a common garb both unifies and separates.

Except in one conservative community, the women wear white organdy head coverings called prayer caps. The style varies from area to area. Over this may be worn a dark-colored bonnet for outdoor wear. The style of dress is of one pattern within an area. It often features a front-bodice closing secured with straight pins. Frequently an apron or pinafore is worn over the dress. Shawls and capes are popular for added protection. If you were an Amish woman, your clothes would all be of one style, one length, year in and year out. The color of the dresses would vary regionally but would be in the Amish palette of colors (see page 13). Clothes become darker as a woman ages. Similarity of dress is to encourage modesty and discourage competition. Women don't cut their hair, wearing it in braids or a bun under the cap. No jewelry, not even a wedding ring, is worn.

There are also regional differences in the garb worn by men. Styles of hats, coats, and trousers vary slightly with area, age, and also season. Sometimes only hooks and eyes are permissible on coats. Adult men have beards, which signify church membership and marriage. Mustaches are not worn.

The Amish goal is to be self-sufficient from the outside world. They don't want to be part of the government structure. They pay taxes, but build and maintain their own schools. They don't collect welfare, pensions, or social security. They won't hold public office, although some of them vote. The Amish are conscientious objectors, serving in hospitals if drafted. They won't go to court if sued, and won't file suit themselves if wronged. Transactions are handled in cash; credit or installment buying is frowned upon.

Life centers around the farm, where most things are done the old way, without the benefit of modern technology. Food, livestock, and a cash crop may be grown. Families are large and close.

Children are given tasks from an early age. Work is an important part of all stages of life. At the time of marriage of the youngest son, the parents build and move into a grandfather's house on the property.

Amish drive horse-drawn buggies, the style of which varies regionally. The buggies are usually black or grey, though two conservative groups in Pennsylvania have white and yellow buggies. Modern labor-saving devices are for the most part deemed unnecessary. Generally the Amish do without electricity and phones; the lines are considered a connection with the outside world. There is a wide variation in what is acceptable, with even forty miles making a difference in practices. The Beachy Amish, for example, drive cars, use modern tractors, and have electricity and telephones. Their clothing may be almost identical to other Amish in the area, but may permit the use of zippers.

Children attend school only through the eighth grade. This provides ample education for the life their parents want them to lead. The Amish teachers have the same education. Much of what the children need to know will be learned firsthand on the farm helping their parents.

Though many other details of Amish life could be discussed here, the important part for us is that the Amish lead a simple life that centers around their religion. Many of the decisions about life are already made for them by their church or have evolved from custom. For example, weddings usually take place in November when the harvest is in, giving more free time. The ceremony takes place on a Tuesday or Thursday so the benches used for Sunday services can be moved to a new house. In this case there's a simple and obvious reason for a practice. Sometimes the reason has become lost and things are merely done out of habit.

Amish families are patriarchal. A woman's concerns are for her family. She is in charge of the house and the garden, which usually includes both vegetables and flowers. She may be involved with clothes production. Amish women often love to embroider and to quilt. As always, since there must be a utilitarian function, the embroidery is done on tea towels and bed linens. Quilts are used for warmth, and are made at times of birth or marriage, and when old ones wear out. Today, many Amish women make quilts to sell to the outside world as a means of supplementing family income; some also quilt tops sewn by others. A grandfather, not wanting to work in the fields anymore, may even help cut out quilt pieces.

A strong tradition of mutual assistance binds the Amish. If a barn is struck by lightning and burns, fellow Amish neighbors will help the farmer rebuild. Much quilting is accomplished the same way. Quilting bees or frolics are often held. Sometimes the participants are chosen in unique ways, such as women born in a particular year or having the same first name.

Many of the quilts made today by the Amish are for the outside world, catering to "English" tastes in calico prints. The quilts we'll be discussing in this book generally were made before 1940. I will be concentrating mainly on Pennsylvania, Ohio, and Indiana quilts. As noted earlier, most of the other Amish settlements came into being after 1940.

I have asserted that quilts are a reflection of the people who make them. This is particularly true for the Amish. The Diamond and Bars quilts are as unique as the Amish themselves. They are simple and unlike any other quilts in the mainstream of American quilting. Even when the Amish work with familiar patterns, their version will be unusual because of their use of only solid colors. Prints are considered too worldly. And as for construction, the wide borders are never mitered, a common practice by other quilters. It's easier not to miter—so the Amish don't.

The color palette is one of the most unusual aspects of Amish quilts. The colors come directly from the clothes they wear. One has only to view clotheslines in an Amish area on Mondays, the traditional washday, to see this. When asked, most people would state that Amish quilts are dark. Upon viewing these quilts in person, the same people are usually surprised by the variety of colors used and the range of values, from very dark to pastel, that may appear in one quilt. Some Amish quilts feature the brightest pure colors, while others are done in greyed, mysterious tones. It's how the colors are combined into one quilt that makes the Amish coloration of quilts so unique.

The color wheel can help you to understand color. When two of the three primary colors—red, yellow, and blue—are mixed together, the secondary colors orange, green, and purple are produced. The colors located between the primary and secondary colors are called tertiary, and combine first the primary name, followed by the secondary

name. The value of an individual color can be changed by adding white so it becomes a tint or pastel, or black to darken it to a shade. For example, baby blue and navy blue are a light and dark value of blue. When both white and black are added, the result is a greyed color (see Figure A.1).

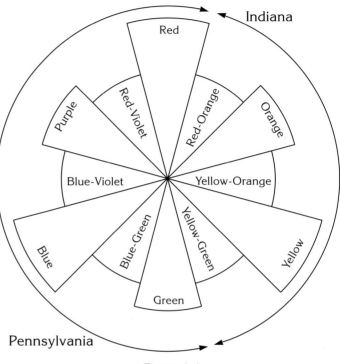

Figure A.1

Many exciting things happen when you start to combine colors. The purpose of this book is to explore some of these happenings. Initially, you'll limit yourself to the Pennsylvania Amish palette of green to red, and the neutral black. Eliminating orange, yellow, and yellow-green will help to guarantee a correct Amish feeling. When the midwestern quilts are dealt with in Lesson 7 on Repeat Block quilts, try adding these colors plus the neutrals tan and brown. The sparkle effect discussed in Lesson 1 is most noticeable in subdued lighting. A good way to check for it is to dim the lights. The Amish lit their homes with kerosene lamps, which produce a subdued light. Perhaps this effect was accidentally discovered, liked, and repeated on purpose without ever verbalizing it.

No one knows for sure why the Amish have chosen to use color as they do. The end result is very strong and powerful. Perhaps that is reason enough. You will find your own work changed after working with Amish colors.

SUGGESTIONS

For your study of Amish quilts, you'll need a good collection of solid-color fabrics. Buy all you can find and afford. Select any color or value that falls within the recommended palette. Black is very important. Buy as many versions as possible. I prefer 100% cotton because it machine stitches better than fabrics which contain polyester. If a large collection is difficult to gather in your area, try mail-order. There are several good firms with fantastic assortments. Check your quilt magazines.

Machine piece your projects. Then you'll be able to take advantage of the speed techniques covered in the Appendix. Make your projects relatively small. It's better to tackle several quilts and go through all the color decisions rather than concentrating on one big project, with only one set of choices to make and to learn from.

Learn to use the rotary cutter. You will save time even if you're only cutting one layer because you eliminate the drawing around the template. Quilters always complain of not having enough time to get their projects done. Using the sewing machine and rotary cutter will give you that time.

Critique your work on the wall. This is a much faster process, and you can see what you're doing so much better because it's all on one plane. Use felt, flannel, or synthetic fleece to cover a wall area. Your fabric pieces will adhere to the surface while you're experimenting. Pin them in place when you are satisfied. This method will also allow you a chance to live with a piece before it's sewn. You'll cut down tremendously on ripping-out time.

I have purposely not included patterns in this book. My intent is to demonstrate how you can make your own patterns and your own color decisions. Refer to the Appendix whenever you need specific help on a procedure. Be sure to study the accompanying pictures for each chapter in the center photo section.

NINE-PATCH

I would like to begin with the Nine-Patch quilt. It's just complex enough to be a challenge. You will also be pleased and amazed with how much you'll discover about color in general, the Amish use of color in particular, and what I feel is the Amish approach to quiltmaking.

Try both exercises in this lesson; you can learn something different from each one. I'm assuming you will be working in order through the book, so if you do choose to skip an exercise, at least read through it for the insights and suggestions presented.

Exercise #1 PLAYING WITH THE BACKGROUND

No Amish quilt looks exactly like our first example (Figure 1.1), but it is inspired by design and color aspects I have found in Amish quilts. In this exercise, we will explore color interaction, asymmetrical placement, and bordering. This first exercise will help you to better understand all the other quilts in the book. No one sentence or even one paragraph will summarize what you need to learn. You can only learn by doing these exercises yourself. So let's begin....

Spread your fabric collection out in front of you. Select three pieces to work with for the background squares. They should be almost the same color (analogous), and of varying (light to medium) values. Perhaps one is more grey, or "dirtier," than the others. Maybe one has more blue in it, another one more red. That is, they are similar but they don't exactly match—in fact, they sort of mismatch. Now you are becoming Amish.

Figure 1.1

Find two other colors to combine with these three. These two—fabrics A and B—will be for the nine-patches. One should be darker than anything you have selected so far; black's an easy choice here. The second color should be of medium value, but not too similar to your three background colors. It shouldn't blend with them.

As you audition the possible combinations, try arranging the fabric as in Figure 1.2. This layout allows you to see how the colors interact.

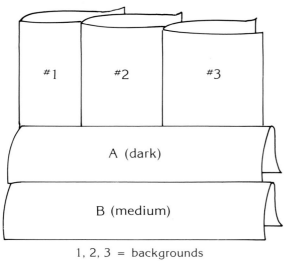

1, 2, 3 = backgrounds
A, B = nine-patches
Figure 1.2

Once you've decided upon a combination, the next step is to make sixteen nine-patches. A nine-patch may be colored in two ways, as indicated in Figure 1.3. The color placement doesn't affect the sewing. The units fit together either way. In traditional American quilts, one arrangement is chosen and then all the nine-patches are assembled having an identical value placement. An Amish Nine-Patch quilt often has both arrangements present. There are always more of the "five dark and four medium or light blocks" (hereafter denoted as 5:4) than the "four dark and five medium or light combinations" (hereafter denoted as 4:5).

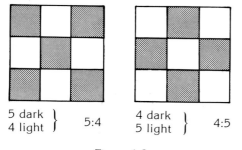

5 dark
4 light } 5:4   4 dark
5 light } 4:5

Figure 1.3

I believe this has to do with visualization capabilities. In teaching quiltmaking, I've noticed some students don't see the difference between the 5:4 and 4:5 blocks until it's pointed out. Quilters who do not know how to draft pieced designs tend to accept pattern pieces with blind faith and often don't understand how the use of value in coloring establishes the visual pattern.

For the most part, Amish quilters were like this. Some women made the same pattern over and over again because that was the set of templates they had. If they wanted to make a new pattern, they would trace it off the quilt on someone else's bed. Obviously a few Amish women knew how to make or draft the patterns, but the majority worked with what was available to them. They would cut out the fabric pieces, making sure that the colors were different from each other, but they didn't necessarily pay attention to the handling of value.

Make sixteen nine-patches from fabrics A and B; to be "Amish" make at least two of the blocks with the 4:5 configuration, but keep the 5:4 blocks in the majority. Don't be tempted to do half of each. Your blocks should look like those in Figure 1.4.

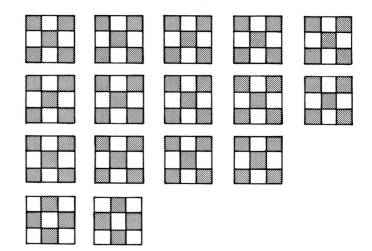

Figure 1.4

Refer to the Appendix for suggestions on a fast way to make your nine-patches. For this exercise, cut your strips 1¼" wide. (These aren't the methods the Amish used, but I'm sure they would have used them if they had known of them!) True-up the nine-patches according to instructions in the Appendix. Deal with the size the blocks actually are rather than the size they should be. Make sure the measurement is a square. This approach is very "Amish."

Using a template the size of your trued-up nine-patches, cut four squares each of colors #1, #2, and #3.

Position your nine-patches as shown in Figure 1.5. You might try pinning them up on the wall as discussed in the Introduction. Ignore where you place the 4:5 blocks. Try not to make their position obvious or symmetrical.

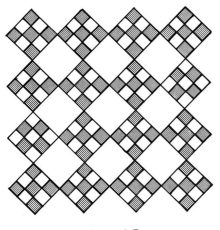

Figure 1.5

Now you are ready to experiment with the placement of the background squares. Make sure all units touch each other so that you will see maximum color interaction. Follow the arrangement used in Figure 1.6.

When a particular color (#1, #2, or #3) is placed in the center position (X), two possible ways remain to arrange the other two colors. As you're

working with the three background colors, there are altogether six possible arrangements (provided you follow the suggestions and don't cheat). Figure 1.7 shows the possibilities.

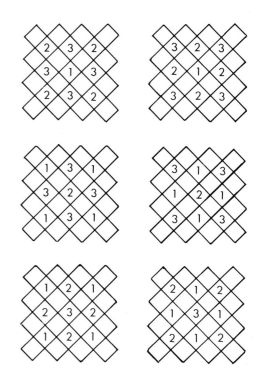

Figure 1.7

At this point you haven't cut the perimeter triangles. However, you can take the three remaining blocks that match the center (X), fold them in half diagonally, and insert them in the correct positions along the bottom of the nine-patch formation. This will help you to visualize the finished arrangement.

As you experiment with the various positions for the background squares, you should see the point of Exercise #1. Colors #1, #2, and #3 seem to change or feel different depending on their placement within the quilt. This is even more noticeable if you're working with greyed rather than pure colors. Two things may be causing this to happen. First, some of the colors may feel lighter or darker as you move them around. Value is how light or dark a color is, and value is relative—it changes according to what else is being used in the project. Surrounding a given color with darker colors will make it appear lighter. Surrounding that same color with lighter ones will make it appear darker.

Second, if you are working with greyed colors, the colors of the blocks may appear to be quite different within the quilt than they did as yardage.

X = color in center, also perimeter triangles
Y = color in corner blocks
Z = color in middle blocks

Figure 1.6

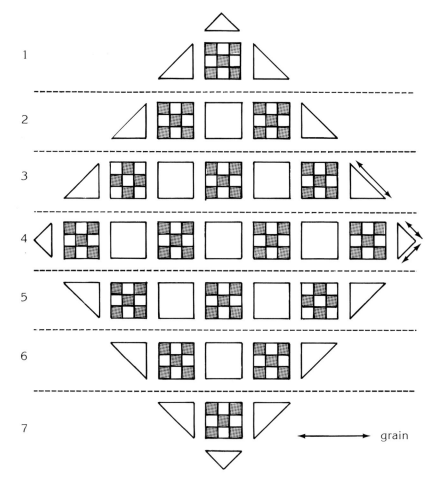

Figure 1.8

This is because colors often have other colors in them. For example, if you have a grey with a green undertone (perhaps not even visible to you when you selected it), and you surround it with red in your quilt, it will appear to be green. Red is green's contrasting color and therefore the green is "pulled out" of the grey fabric. Both of these ideas are exciting because in effect they increase the size of your physical fabric collection. You can make fabrics darker or lighter by what you place around them. You can even change the color of some fabrics by experimenting with what you combine with them. Once you see this second phenomenon happen, you'll be able to identify other pieces of yardage that potentially will change for you. Often you will find it hard to give a name to these colors. They appear "dirty" in contrast to pure colors.

Select the color arrangement you like the best. To assemble the quilt top, cut twelve perimeter triangles and four corner triangles (check the Appendix for details). To ensure that your quilt top doesn't stretch, cut the triangles with the outside edge(s) on grain.

Assemble the top into rows; then join rows. By pressing the seam allowance into the background blocks, you'll always have the seam allowances in opposite directions (Figure 1.8) as you sew one row to another. This will reduce bulk at the joining points.

BORDERING

Amish quilts are known for their wide outer borders; they usually have a narrow inner border between this and the central design. Sometimes there are corner blocks in the wide border. Corner blocks may also be present within the narrow border. Figure 1.9 shows all these variations.

Pennsylvania Amish quilts, which are usually square, have the widest borders, often with the big corner blocks. They usually have the narrow inner border which sometimes contains corner blocks. Ohio and Indiana Amish quilts, which are usually

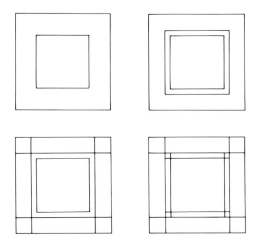

Figure 1.9

rectangular, have a more narrow outer border and often include the narrow inner border. Rarely do they feature the corner blocks.

Unfortunately, an easy formula doesn't exist to tell us which format or colors to use. However, I've discovered that the quilt itself can aid you in this decision. Place your quilt top on the wall. For Exercise #1, restrict your possible border color choices to the five colors already in the quilt top. Let's assume that you will have a wide outer border and a narrow inner border.

Audition the five colors with the quilt top (Figure 1.10). Concern yourself first with the narrow inner border. Notice that you cannot use the color that

was used for the perimeter triangles, as it merely blends in and doesn't outline the quilt top. So the quilt eliminated one choice. Eliminate any others which blend too much.

Now audition the remaining possibilities for the inner narrow border with the five fabrics again to choose a wide outer border. Try to expose the amount of fabric which feels right each time. This gets easier with practice. You can hold up your right hand to shield from view the right side of the arrangement where there's excess fabric. Your extended thumb can shield the bottom from view. A width that is too wide usually overpowers the design area. A width that is too narrow will look skimpy.

When you have selected both your inner and outer borders, test to see if the quilt needs corner blocks in the wide border. Superimpose the candidates over the upper left-hand corner. Some quilts seem to need this finishing touch. Other borders are strong enough already and don't need the additional help of corner blocks (Figure 1.11).

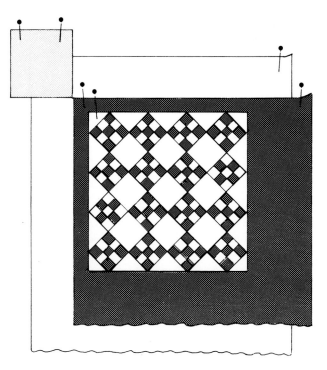

Figure 1.11

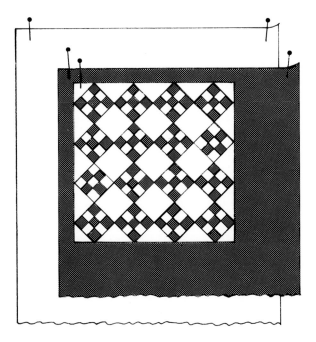

Figure 1.10

Sew the borders on your quilt. Refer to the Appendix for cutting and sewing suggestions.

One final thought: eventually you will need to choose a binding. To be Amish, choose a fabric that you haven't already used in the quilt. Often it's related, but may be one shade darker or a little greyer. Maybe it will have a shine. Sometimes the quilt needs a little spark. This is your last opportunity to make a statement. Refer to the Appendix for suggestions on cutting and sewing the binding.

Exercise #2 *SPARKLE*

When you look at Amish Double Nine-Patch quilts, you will discover that many of them have a wonderful sparkling appearance, almost like twinkling stars. To emulate this idea, you can make a simplified version of the Double Nine-Patch which will be faster and easier to sew but will produce the same result (Figure 1.12).

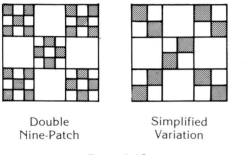

Double   Simplified
Nine-Patch   Variation

Figure 1.12

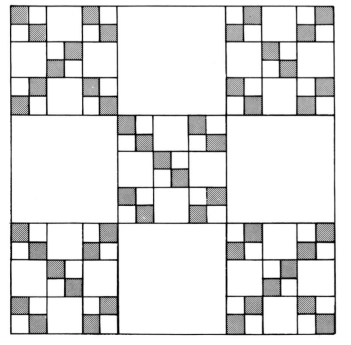

Figure 1.13

Divide your fabric collection into piles with dark, medium, and light values. Momentarily forget about color and concentrate on value. Start with the obvious ones first. It's usually easiest to identify light and dark; those remaining should be medium. Move fabrics back and forth between the piles until you decide where the fabric feels most at home. Eliminate any that are confusing.

To do Exercise #2 you will need to make a minimum of twenty-five four-patches. Again, check the Appendix for details on this process. These will join together to form five double nine-patches (Figure 1.13). Make five duplicates of each combination rather than five different examples of each combination. You will only need to select five color sets:

Number of Sets	Value + Value	
one	dark + dark	
one	dark + medium	*Boring*
one	medium + medium	*Blocks*
one	medium + greyed light	
one	dark + clear light } *Sparkle Blocks*	

You will be making "Sparkle" blocks and what I call "Boring" blocks. If all the blocks sparkle, the effect isn't noticeable. It's only when there are boring, dull blocks to serve as a contrast to the blocks that sparkle that you will notice the twinkling effect. "Sparkle" blocks must be less than half of the total used.

It's easiest to start with the "Boring" blocks. Choose four sets. Combine any two fabrics in the dark pile, making sure you can see a difference in value between the two. Next, combine another dark with a medium. Now combine two mediums. If they are of equal value, they will "fade away" in an interesting way. Finally, combine a medium with a greyed light.

To make "Sparkle" blocks, take a dark and combine it with a pale, clear light (as opposed to greyed light). The "Sparkle" effect is maximized when there's the greatest difference in value between the two fabrics used. A medium combined with a clear light will not sparkle as much. In Exercise #1 you learned that the way to lighten a color is to surround it with a darker one. Make a "Sparkle" combination set.

Don't recycle the same fabrics in various combinations, but select new fabrics. Don't be tempted to combine sets in a traditional American approach of two values of one color such as red and pink or navy blue with light blue. Your color combinations should feel like they "mismatch" rather than co-ordinate.

Sew the four-patches, as described in the Appendix. Next select the fabric which will join the four-patches to create the double nine-patches. Greyed fabrics in the light-to-medium range seem to work well. Choose candidates from your collection. It isn't necessary to eliminate a color already used. The resulting bleeding effect is very "Amish." Arrange some of the four-patches on each of these to see which fabric works best to join the elements together. The plain blocks shouldn't be more noticeable than the four-patches (Figure 1.14).

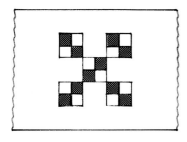

Figure 1.14

True-up the four-patches (see Appendix). Make a template this size for the joining blocks. Cut the necessary number using this pattern, then join to form double nine-patches. Don't be too concerned with placement. The "Sparkle" blocks should be placed at random. Even the dark-light placement within the four-patches should be randomly arranged. (Refer to Figure 1.13.)

Next, audition the fabric for the large alternate blocks between the double nine-patches. Use the same method. Greyed fabrics are easiest to use but they aren't the only choice. There should be a difference in value from the fabric already used for the joining blocks within the double nine-patches to help keep the units separate from each other. Again, you may repeat a fabric appearing within the four-patches, which will result in an accidental visual bleeding.

Before sewing the units together, consider placing the blocks on point. Visually the work will look much more complex. This is because you must turn your head on the side to clearly see how the piece is constructed. Study the photographs of the double nine-patches. (See Photos 2A and 2C in color section.)

Once you've decided upon the arrangement, sew the top together. (Refer to Exercise #1.)

Now you are ready to border. Pennsylvania Double Nine-Patches follow the rule of being square and have both inner and outer borders. They may have corner blocks. The rectangular Ohio and Indiana Double Nine-Patches don't have the corner blocks and seem to have slightly narrower outer borders. Follow the method for border selection discussed in Exercise #1. This time you'll be working with a greater choice of colors. You can also add additional colors, in the Amish fashion, if you feel they are needed. Don't use your favorite color just out of habit. Try to select a combination which really enhances what you've done so far. Try everything, even colors you don't think will work. You may be in for a surprise.

ROMAN STRIPES

A Roman Stripes quilt is very easy to construct and provides a wonderful opportunity to play with fabric in a spontaneous way. Rarely is an Amish Roman Stripes unsuccessful, mainly because black is used for the solid triangle half of the block (Figure 2.1). Black is very powerful and tends to bind together anything used with it. Therefore, you can combine almost any set of colors and have the finished product look good. Remember though, not to use the forbidden section of the color wheel discussed in the Introduction when selecting the other colors for your quilt.

Figure 2.1

Exercise #1 **STANDARD ROMAN STRIPES**

Select any six colors, except black, from your collection. For this first set, work only with medium and dark values. Try to have some selections bright, maybe some dull.

Your fabric must be cut into strips of equal width. The width of the strips, the number of strips used within each block, and the number of blocks used within the quilt will determine the size of the finished quilt.

Figure 2.2

For this first, simple example, I suggest you work with strips cut 1" wide (½" sewn). Altogether there will be six strips for each of the twelve blocks. The finished quilt, including borders, will be about 21"x 25" (Figure 2.2).

Strips should be cut the width of the fabric (see Appendix). Cut one strip of each color. Cut these strips in half so that they are now 22" rather than 44" wide. (Don't cut strips of a wider width in half.) Make two piles of strips. Each pile should contain one strip of each color. Now arrange both piles in a different order. Any order will do, just so they don't match. Sew the strips from each pile together (see Appendix) as indicated in Figure 2.3.

1
2
3
4
5
6

3
1
2
5
6
4

Figure 2.3

Make another set of six colors. Repeat four of the colors you have already used and add two replacements (Figure 2.4). One of the new choices should be a clear, light value if you want a little sparkle (Lesson 1, Exercise #2). Remember to work only with 22" strips for this example. (Quilts with wider strips and/or more blocks will require more sewn stripes.)

2
1
7*
3
4
8*

Figure 2.4

You are now ready to draft a triangle template. Measure the height (H) of the sewn stripes (Figure 2.5), and subtract from the height ½" (seam allowance of the two outside edges). The formula is: H – ½" = X, where X equals the finished size.

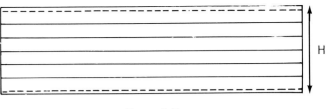

Figure 2.5

Draw a horizontal straight line on the template material. Bisect this line with a perpendicular line. The two lines meet at A. Measure out from A the distance of X in all three directions. Draw lines between the X's to form a triangle. Add ¼" seam allowance to all edges and you have your template. Look carefully at Figure 2.6.

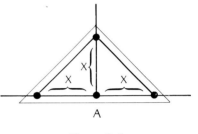

Figure 2.6

Using the template, cut triangles from your stripes. You should get four or five from each stripe. Half of the triangles will be upside-down. There will be two variations from each stripe. For this quilt, there will be a total of six variations (Figure 2.7).

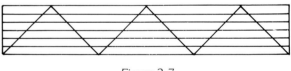

Figure 2.7

Also cut triangles from your black fabric. Using more than one black fabric will enhance the scrap feeling of your quilt. You will need twelve black triangles and twelve striped triangles for this example. Join the striped triangles to the solid triangles to form the blocks.

Using the wall, experiment with placement. You need to consider both the arrangement of the blocks and which way you want the blocks turned. Your narrow inner border should be a new color, perhaps something bright and bold which will hold everything together. Your final wide border should be black for this example.

Figure 2.8

VARIATIONS
Working with a larger number of blocks opens up all sorts of design layout variations. The following exercises also provide some different layouts.

Exercise #2 ROMAN STRIPE ON POINT

Place the blocks on point (Figure 2.8). Additional partial blocks will be needed to fill out the resulting square or rectangle. (See Appendix.) Don't forget that these triangles will need to be specifically made using a template. It is not enough to merely cut an already-made block in half, as seam allowance must be added on the new edge.

Exercise #3 BULL'S-EYE ROMAN STRIPE

Rotate the blocks so that the striped areas come together to form a bull's-eye (Figure 2.9). Consider playing a game with the solid triangles. Work with three different values or colors. In this case, the solid triangles and the striped triangles are arranged on the wall before they are sewn together. Each visual square that contains the solid triangles should only contain two different fabrics, matching colors positioned opposite from each other. When you're ready to sew, seam solid triangles to striped triangles as before.

Exercise #4 CHEVRON ROMAN STRIPE

Another variation (Figure 2.10) results if the blocks are turned to give a zigzag appearance. This variation is called Chevron.

Figure 2.9

Figure 2.10

BRICKS

Bricks is a fairly rare Amish pattern. See Photos 5A and 5B. This will be made as a scrap quilt. Here's an opportunity to work on being more spontaneous, in the Amish fashion. The exercise may be painful for the average quilter but it will help you to take a more spontaneous approach on future projects.

Exercise #1 BRICKS

The Bricks pattern is composed of rectangles whose height is twice their width. For this exercise, work with a finished unit of 1½" x 3". Using the strip cutting method (see Appendix), make strips 2" wide (1½" finished measurement). Keeping the strip folded in fourths, cut three 3½" segments (3" finished measurement). This will give you twelve bricks per strip. Figure 3.1 shows this process clearly.

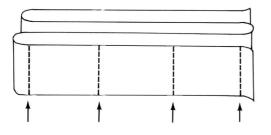

Figure 3.1

Cut one strip from each color in your collection. You want as many choices as possible. Be most sparing with the clear lights. Cut bricks from the strips. Make piles of each fabric, stacking similar colors in close proximity, like an artist's palette.

Again, it's helpful to work on the wall. Each row will stair-step down the quilt, with units meeting at the midpoint of the previous unit (Figure 3.2). The second color choice begins on top of the second block in Row #1. It will temporarily extend above this unit. Row #3 begins above the third unit in Row #2. Later, units that extend beyond the boundary will be cut to the correct size.

Randomly make color choices. At this point each row will contain only one color. To hold the quilt together visually, make every third, fourth, or fifth row black. Keep going until your work is twenty units wide and six units high (Figure 3.3). Fill in the necessary units to complete the rectangle. Stand back and look at what you've done so far.

If you're satisfied, you're ready for the next stage. This step can be both exciting and a little frightening if you tend to be very controlled in what you do. You're ready to "interfere" with what you have just done.

One row at a time, try to replace some of the units with bricks of the same, or almost the same,

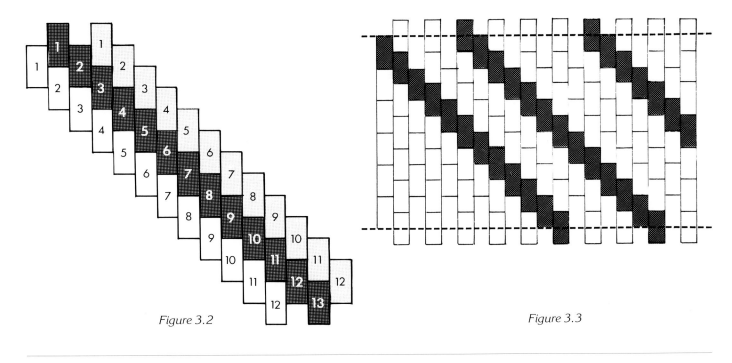

Figure 3.2

Figure 3.3

color. Try playing with value changes, or subtle color changes, or with the degree of greyness. Attempt to be unpredictable with your interference. For example, don't always change three units in order in a row. Or don't always go dark, medium, and light. Even make changes within your black rows by taking advantage of your black collection. Sneak in some grey or a shiny black fabric.

Amish women don't really intentionally "interfere" in their quilts. I feel that in approaching a scrap quilt, the Amish quilter is at ease with making do with what she has on hand. She doesn't feel the rigidity with which we seem to be ingrained. We can learn from this casualness. Our quilts can be much more exciting if we can learn the idea of working with fabrics which don't quite "match," or of combining greyed with clear colors, or of combining brights with dulls.

When you're satisfied with your quilt, prepare to sew it together. Make a template for the half units. Use this to recut the units which extend beyond the boundary of the piece (Figure 3.4).

The quilt can be sewn together in vertical rows. Carefully remove one row at a time, being sure to keep it in order. Pin the sewn row back in the right position on the wall. Remove the next vertical row, sew, and return. Continue until all of the rows have been sewn. Now join the vertical rows together, matching seams to midpoints. It's safest to mark the midpoint rather than relying on your eye (Figure 3.5).

When choosing your narrow border, try to select a color that doesn't touch a perimeter edge; this avoids visual bleeding. Pick a bold, strong color. Black is a good choice for your outer border. Remember that the quilt is rectangular (Ohio and Indiana), so don't make the border too wide.

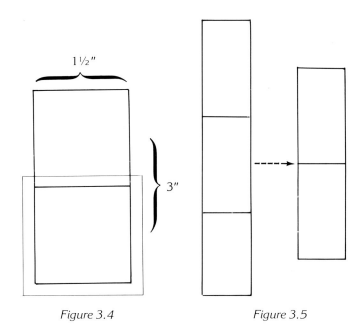

Figure 3.4

Figure 3.5

SUNSHINE AND SHADOW

✛

Sunshine and Shadow is a Pennsylvania Amish quilt, and is rarely done by Amish in other states. The pattern is called Trip Around the World when sewn by non-Amish, or "English." Even though the quilt is structured identically (except for the wide Amish borders), the use of color is quite different between the two groups. The English version would probably contain printed fabrics; these tend to soften the visual impact of the design. The Amish version, of course, is done only in solid colors; these give a far more dramatic result. This, and the use of shading within the Amish version, make it so special and different.

Exercise #1 SHADING (Method #1)

Sort your fabric collection into piles of primary and secondary colors. Within each color pile further divisions representing the variations or tertiary colors will probably develop. (Refer to the Introduction.) For each subgroup, try to find a dark, a medium, and a light to represent shades and tints of that one color. Remember shades are a color plus black, and tints are a color plus white. Some of the light clear colors may actually be able to do service in several nearby piles. It helps to stack the fabrics on each other as you test for the smoothest transitions (Figure 4.1).

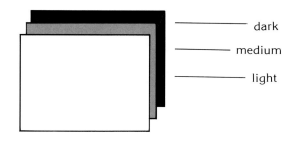

Figure 4.1

You'll need a minimum of three, but preferably four sets. To check if your choices will look good together in a Sunshine and Shadow quilt, make a glued mock-up. Work with ½" squares of each color. Trim ½" off the selvage edge (you don't use this anyway); then further cut these strips to form the necessary squares. To keep some sanity to this operation, store the matching squares in muffin tins or egg cartons.

You'll need a piece of white paper or poster board; working on any other color will distort what you're seeing. You'll also need a glue stick, as wet glue will change the color of the fabric. It's less messy to glue the paper in the desired area than to glue the fabric pieces. Glued squares may be pulled up and replaced.

Start your Sunshine and Shadow mock-up in the middle. There are several ways to color, or

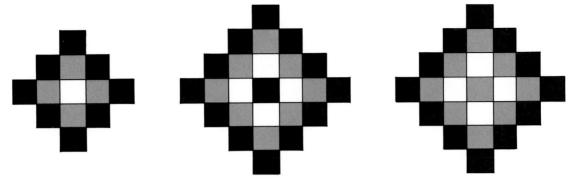

Figure 4.2

shade, this area. Remember, you can change this area after you work your way out to the edges if it no longer feels right. It's really just a matter of needing something there in order to begin your shading series. You are working out to a dark or black row (Figure 4.2).

Amish-style shading is created by working with the following sequences:

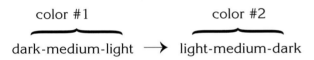

A sequence may contain more than three values of each color. Using this sequence format will give a rolling effect because different values appear on different visual planes. Positioning black (the maximum dark) between the darks of an ending sequence and the darks of a new sequence heightens the effect.

Work out from the middle section you've already created. Remember to place the squares right next to each other so that maximum color interaction will occur.

Plan on about fifteen to nineteen rows in your final Sunshine and Shadow quilt. It isn't necessary to make a glued mock-up of the entire piece; the top half will give you the idea (Figure 4.3).

For a wallhanging-sized quilt, work with 1" to 2" (finished size) units. This quilt can be strip pieced by prefabbing sequences (check the Appendix). Don't include more than three or four strips in a unit. In the correct order, seam prefab units together to form rows. These rows will then be joined in the correct order to complete the top.

Because this is a Pennsylvania quilt (square), you'll have the option of corner blocks in your bor-

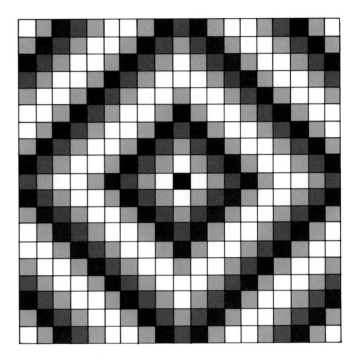

Figure 4.3

ders. Try not to include a color that appears on the perimeter of the design grid for your first color choice.

Exercise #2 SHADING (Method #2)

An alternate method can be used to shade a Sunshine and Shadow quilt. When joining two shaded sequences, attach the dark end of the first sequence to the light end of the second sequence. That is, opposite values are joined rather than matching values. A nice glow will radiate from the light fabric. Remember a value becomes lighter when placed next to a darker value (Figure 4.4).

Figure 4.4

the color appears in a square. This variation is more time-consuming to sew because triangles must be placed at the beginning and end of each row to square off the edge (Figure 4.5).

Exercise #3 DIAMOND GRID

So far the individual units have been positioned parallel to the edges of the quilt. The color appears in a diamond. Instead, turn the units on point. Now

Figure 4.5

DIAMOND

✚

Most people associate the Diamond quilt, along with both Bars and Sunshine and Shadow patterns, with the Amish. The Diamond is perhaps the most unique when compared to the mainstream of American quiltmaking. Why is it so simple? Where did the idea for the pattern come from?

The Diamond is a Pennsylvania quilt, specifically from Lancaster County. The Amish who lived there tended to be conservative. Those who wanted a less restricted life moved to other areas such as Ohio, Indiana, or Missouri. They discontinued use of this pattern in their new surroundings.

In the second half of the last century, quilters took great pride in the number of pieces they had in a quilt. It was a way to compete with their peers. Since the Amish aren't supposed to display excessive pride, this might explain the simplicity of this quilt. There's also speculation that the Amish hymnal, or *Ausbund*, which has a similar format for the cover design, may have been the inspiration. No one knows for sure. However, early Canadian quilts made from hand woven ginghams and plaids also used this format, as well as some Welsh quilts. Perhaps this is really just a common early quilt form.

Accept the simplicity of the Amish Diamond and use it as a tool to explore color. Because it is so simple to construct and sew, you can quickly make some samples. Even consider working in

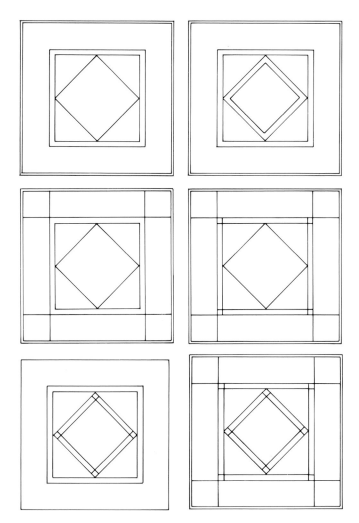

Figure 5.1

31

miniature, which will use a very small amount of fabric.

The quilt has a center square turned on point. This diamond may have narrow borders. Triangles bring the diamond back to a square. Narrow and wide borders are added. There may be corner blocks within either or both of these borders. Quilts without the corner blocks in the wide border are said to "float" (Figure 5.1).

Working with a 5½" square (finished 5") for the center will give you about a 12" finished top, perfect for a pillow. To draft the triangles, draw an X in a 5" square (finished size). Add seam allowance to one of the triangles (Figure 5.2). For the border, check the Appendix for instructions.   Remember to experiment with colors. Set yourself some goals

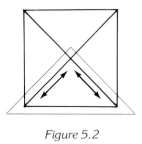

Figure 5.2

and then see if you can make them happen. Make one quilt with all Crayola® hues, or try combining greyed colors with a clear bright. Make one version with all mysterious, murky fabrics; try other variations by positioning the same fabrics in different places.

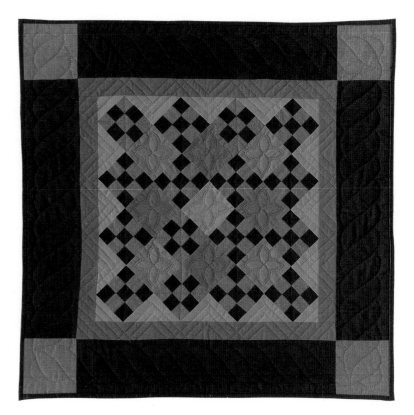

A

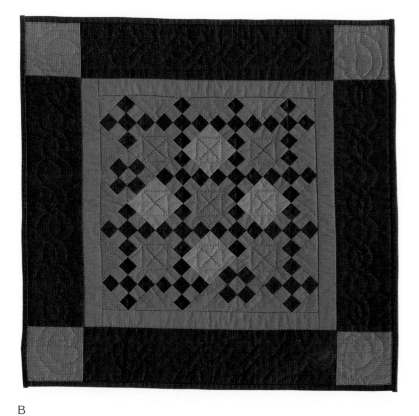

B

1
Nine-Patch

A   Nine-Patch
    27" x 27"
    Joan Dyer
    Redondo Beach, CA

B   Nine-Patch
    21" x 21"
    Roberta Horton
    Berkeley, CA

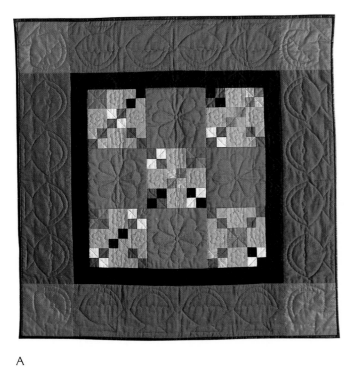

A

B

2
Nine-Patch

A   Double Nine-Patch
    32" x 32"
    Carolyn Hartsough
    Berkeley, CA

B   Nine-Patch
    24" x 28"
    George Taylor
    Anchorage, AK

C   Tears (Double Nine-Patch)
    42" x 42"
    Sandra Forman
    Palos Verdes Estates, CA

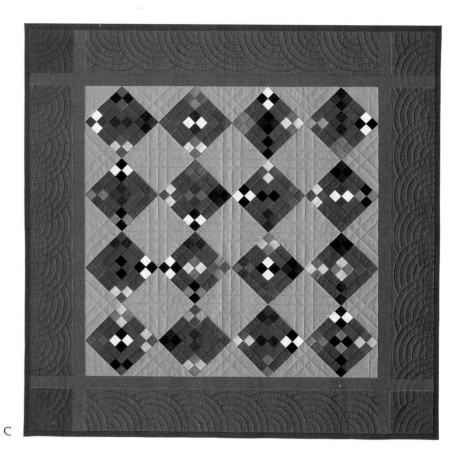

C

A

B

C

3
Roman Stripes

A   Roman Stripes
    23" x 28"
    Carolyn Hartsough
    Berkeley, CA

B   Roman Stripe Variation
    29" x 30"
    Mary Helen Schwyn
    Walnut Creek, CA

C   Roman Strip Variation
    33" x 37"
    Claudia Alldredge
    Berkeley, CA

A

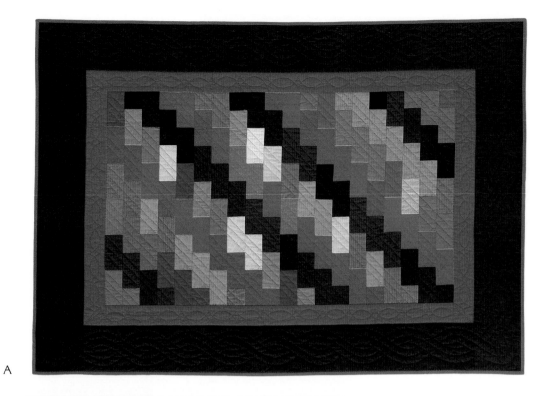

A

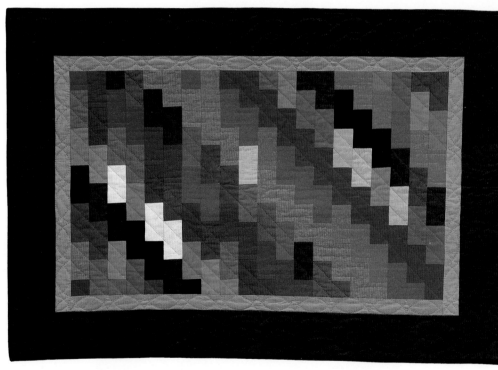

B

4 *Facing Page*
Roman Stripes

A   Roman Stripe Variation
    78" x 96"
    Miriam Nathan-Roberts
    Berkeley, CA
    quilting by
    Ladies of the Night

5
Bricks

A   Bricks
    41" x 29"
    Nadi Lane
    Agoura, CA

B   Bricks
    39" x 27"
    Helen Temple Cummins
    Carmichael, CA

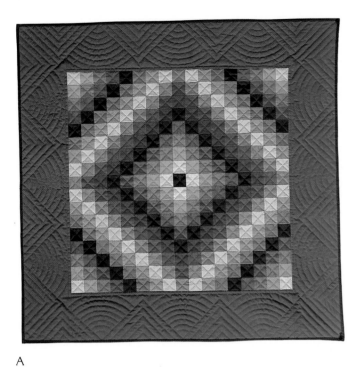

A

B

6
Sunshine and Shadow

A Sunshine and Shadow
   42" x 42"
   Gai Perry
   Walnut Creek, CA

B Sunshine and Shadow
   48" x 48"
   Claudia Alldredge
   Berkeley, CA
   Over-dyed fabrics

C Sunshine and Shadow Variation
   40" x 40"
   Joan Ellis
   Berkeley, CA

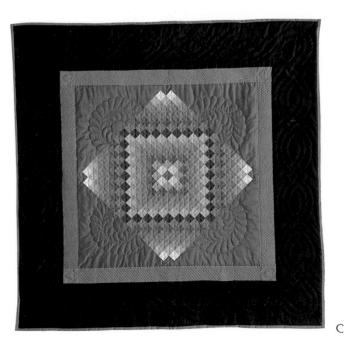

C

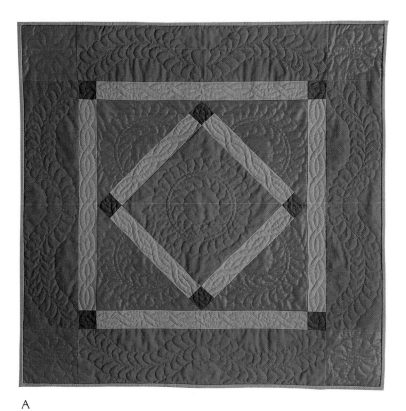

A

B   C

D

7
Diamond and Bars

A Diamond
   39" x 39"
   Carolyn Hartsough
   Berkeley, CA

B Bars
   7¼" x 6⅝"
   Constance Kossa
   Berkeley, CA

C Bars
   6" x 6½"
   Constance Kossa
   Berkeley, CA

D Bars
   31" x 32"
   Carolyn Harsough
   Berkeley, CA

A

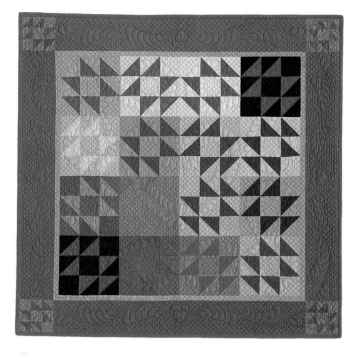

B

8
Repeat

A   Old Maid's Puzzle
    27" x 35"
    Janet Shore
    El Cerrito, CA

B   Diamonds for Kyle (Double X)
    48" x 48"
    Bonnie Bucknam Holmstrand
    Anchorage, AK

C   Shoo-Fly
    46" x 56"
    Cynthia Corbin
    Woodinville, WA

C

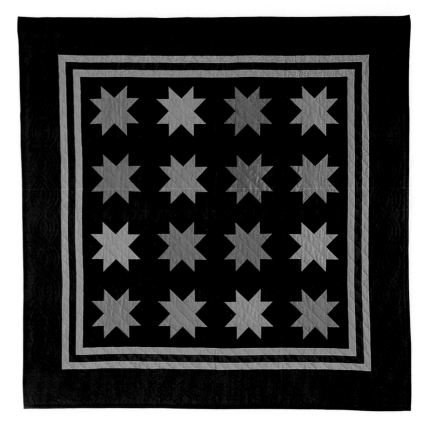

A

B

9
Repeat Block

A Eight-Pointed Star
   56" x 56"
   Cathie Hoover
   Modesto, CA

B Bear's Paw
   54" x 54"
   Judy Mullen
   Manteca, CA

A

10
Repeat Block

A   Pinwheel
    35" x 42"
    Susan Arnold
    Berkeley, CA

B   Pinwheels Gone Awry
    55" x 55"
    Miriam Nathan-Roberts,
    © 1983
    Berkeley, CA
    quilting by
    Sarah Hershberger
    Charm, Ohio

B

A

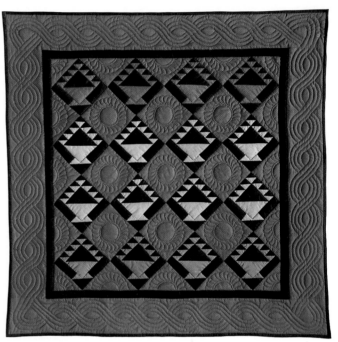

B

C

11
Baskets

A Baskets with Chips
    34" x 41"
    Constance Kossa
    Berkeley, CA

B Baskets
    38" x 39"
    Barbara Dallas
    Portland, OR

C Baskets
    23" x 23"
    Joan Dawson
    Bothell, WA

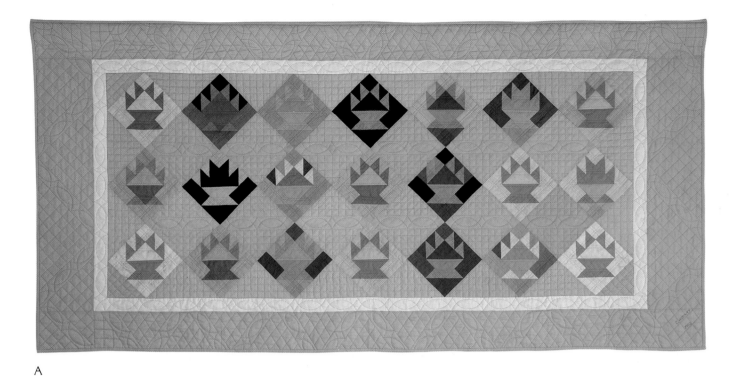

A

12
Baskets

A   Baskets
75" x 37"
Cathie Hoover
Modesto, CA

B   Indiana Flower Baskets
39" x 46"
Cynthia Corbin
Woodinville, WA

13 *Facing Page*
Baskets

A   Indiana Baskets
55" x 65"
Roberta Horton
Berkeley, CA
quilting by Mary Mashuta
Berkeley, CA

B

A

45

A

B

14
Challenge

A   Nine-Patch
    Barn Raising design
    35" x 39"
    Susan McNally
    Walnut Creek, CA

B   Cross-in-the-Square
    42" x 51"
    Gai Perry
    Walnut Creek, CA

C   Nine-Patch
    24" x 28"
    Elizabeth Stypes
    Walnut Creek, CA

C

A

B

15
Challenge

A   Four-Patch Variation
    56" x 56"
    Jane Toro
    El Cerrito, CA

B   Mock-ups for
    Challenge Exercise
    Jane Toro

A

16
Ocean Waves

A   Ocean Waves
    40" x 30"
    Gai Perry
    Walnut Creek, CA

B   Ocean Waves
    41" x 32"
    Roberta Horton
    Berkeley, CA

B

BARS

Bars is the third well-known Pennsylvania Amish quilt. It features narrow inner and wide outer borders and frequently has corner blocks. It's also a very simple quilt to construct, ideal for experimentation. Bars have five, seven, or nine narrow strips in the quilt center. Width is controlled by the number of strips, with the nine-bar version being the only true square (Figure 6.1). There are usually a minimum of three colors used, although a few only have two colors.

Think small. If you go to a 6" finished top, consider using ⅛" seam allowances. Experiment with spray starching your fabric; the fabric will be much more manageable when you machine stitch. If you use water-soluble marking pens to mark your templates, spray, iron, and then mark to prevent bleeding from the pen.

Exercise #1 STANDARD BARS

Try some experimenting with color. To make the bars seemingly float above the quilt, make the wide borders and the alternate even-numbered bars within the center the same color. Choose a second color for the odd-numbered bars and the corner blocks, and a third color for the inner narrow border. The second and third colors should be of contrasting value to the first (Figure 6.2).

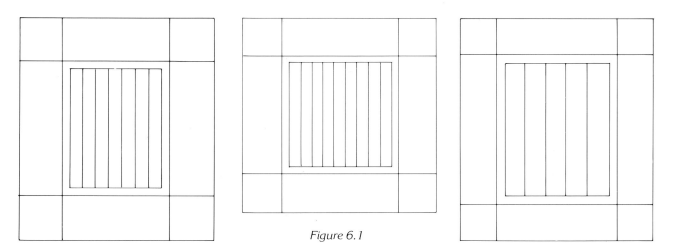

Figure 6.1

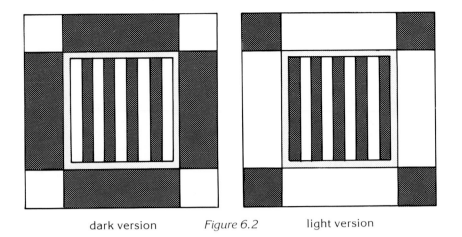

dark version   *Figure 6.2*   light version

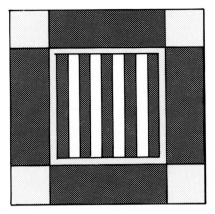

Figure 6.3

To make it appear as if you can see behind the bars, make the outer border and the odd bars the same dark color. The even bars should be of a lighter value (Figure 6.3).

It's also possible to make sections of the quilt seem to glow. This is known as translucence. The quilt must be dark, that is, composed of fabrics which contain black. Either some of the bars or the inner border must then be a pure (clear) color. The quilt will appear to be lit up from within.

Exercise #2 **SPLIT BARS**

Sometimes these bars themselves may be split, hence the name. Either all the odd or all the even bars are split into three equal parts (Figure 6.4). The splitting presents even more of a challenge in terms of color.

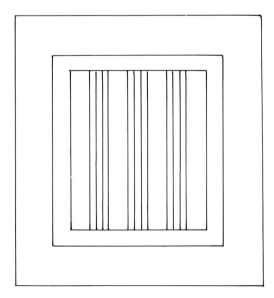

Figure 6.4

Exercise #3 **CHINESE COINS**

You can also break up the odd-numbered bars into squares of different colors, a pattern known as Chinese Coins (Figure 6.5).

Figure 6.5

Exercise #4 **ROMAN COINS**

For this pattern, every other bar should be composed of varicolored strips (Figure 6.6).

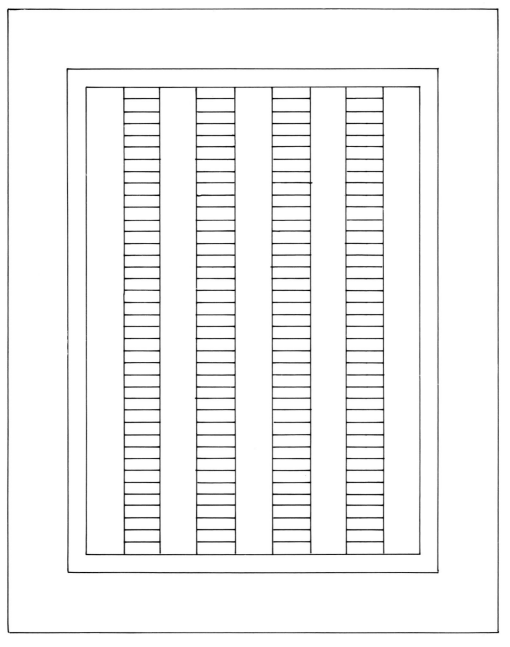

Figure 6.6

REPEAT BLOCK

Quilts made outside of Pennsylvania rely heavily on what I call the repeat block format. This type of quilt is composed of one design repeated to make the quilt the desired size. Perhaps because these Amish often had more interaction with their "English" neighbors, they adopted what has become the formula for the traditional American quilt. The use of the inner and outer border continues, but now the outer border is narrower than the style of Pennsylvania. Corner blocks are omitted, and quilts are more often rectangular rather than square.

The special Amish color palette is broadened. Midwestern Amish seem to work with all colors, even occasionally producing some pastel, light-colored quilts. New colors include orange and yellow and the neutrals: tan, beige, brown, and grey. Black and navy are seen frequently for the background (field). Indiana Amish quilts also seem to feature yellow-greens and golds. Hint: Eliminate red-violet or magenta when you work with yellow-green.

To emulate the correct Amish approach, work within these restrictions:

- Use the same pattern for all the design blocks within the quilt.
- Use only two colors within each individual block.
- Coloration may vary from block to block within the quilt, as long as only two colors appear in each individual block.

A number of patterns were commonly used by the Amish for their Repeat Block quilts. Most feature right-angle triangles (Figure 7.1). Refer to the Appendix for help in drafting these patterns to the desired size and for a quick method to produce the half-of-a-square triangles.

Squares and rectangles can be added to the half-of-a-square triangles to produce more complex designs, as in Figure 7.2. Two blocks can

Pinwheel

Figure 7.1

Double X

Figure 7.2

Old Maid's Puzzle

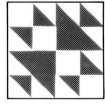

Bowtie Variation

Figure 7.3

contain identical geometric shapes, but they may be arranged or rotated to produce two distinct versions. In this case, both patterns would have different names (Figure 7.3).

The Amish were quite casual about naming their quilts; multiple versions of each pattern exist. In addition to those already shown, five other designs are frequently repeated. See Figure 7.4 for four of those designs. Basket blocks, which are also repeat patterns, will be covered in Lesson 8.

Shoo-Fly

Hole-in-the-Barn-Door

Bear's Paw

Stars
FOUR-PATCH

Stars
NINE-PATCH
Figure 7.4

The following variations cover several basic ways to set the blocks into the quilt once they've been constructed. Also consider whether you want your blocks on point. Remember many designs look more complex this way. Some designs, however, don't read well on point.

Exercise #1 ADJACENT BLOCKS

Blocks can be placed adjacent to each other. This sounds simple, but can actually be very exciting, because unexpected things sometimes happen. The repeated blocks can create an overall pattern unpredictable from one block; or multiple patterns can emerge within the quilt. Photos 8A, 8B and 8C show this effect.

An exciting direction to pursue is varying color among the repeat blocks. This was often done by the Amish because they were frequently working with scraps. This also accidentally happened because many of the Midwestern quilts were made with cotton sateen, a fabric with a directional sheen. Different colors result if the grain is turned, just as can happen with corduroy.

This method may at first be hard to do on purpose. However, it's a necessary step for color growth, and is very Amish. It is also very much in the right feeling to have some of the blocks not clearly defined. More about this in the next lesson. This is accomplished by using two different colors that happen to be the same value. The block then lacks the correct value difference that contrasts the pattern and the background. Seen from afar, it's a disappearing block; up close, the pattern shows because two different colors are used.

Do a glued mock-up to explore the possibilities with color. Select one background color from which you cut 2" squares (Photo 8C required twelve, Photo 8B required sixteen). Place these next to each other as they would be arranged in the finished quilt. This is boring!

Now try to make the background composition interesting by replacing some of the squares with other fabrics. Work first with variations of the original color such as darker, lighter, or shinier. Also experiment with adding other colors. When you're pleased with the results, glue the squares down on paper and proceed to the next step.

Cut 1⅜" squares to represent the design colors. Arrange these on point on the background squares until you are satisfied with the combinations

Figure 7.5

(Figure 7.5). You can have some duplicate combinations or clones (Figure 7.5). Try for a sparkle block and also a fade-out block. Remember not to combine two values of one color for a block but instead, mismatch. Glue in place when you're pleased with the results.

Finally, audition the inner and outer borders. Start with an outer border color that most represents your background squares. The inner border may be a brand-new color not used in the interior of the quilt. Play with various combinations until you find the most exciting results. Cut and glue.

You now have a mock-up that will serve as a blueprint for your finished quilt. You know the two colors that will be used in each block and the sewn order of the finished blocks. The 2" square represents the background and the 1⅜" diamond represents the pattern area. Merely select your pattern and construct your quilt in the desired size.

Exercise #2 **LATTICE**

A dividing strip or lattice can be added when the blocks are joined. (See Appendix.) If all the blocks have identical background color and the color of the lattice is also the same, the contrasting color

sections of the blocks will "float" above the background field. Study Photo 9A. When the design blocks have backgrounds of different colors, then the lattice will have to be of a color strong enough to hold the composition together. In this case, the lattice would both separate the blocks from each other and hold them together.

Exercise #3 **ALTERNATE BLOCKS**

Plain alternate blocks can be interspersed between the design blocks. As with the use of a lattice, if the background of the design blocks and the alternate blocks are from the same fabric, then the designs will "float." Or vary the color in each background among the repeat blocks and also among the plain alternate squares.

Exercise #4 **NEW DIRECTIONS**

Repeat Block offers an opportunity to experiment and perhaps go beyond "Traditional Amish." Photo 10A shows a good example of ignoring the rule allowing two colors within a block. The quilt is far more interesting because the rule has been broken. Photo 10B has gone even further and is an exciting example of what we might call "Contemporary Amish." The borders have been dropped. The color palette is Amish, but more than two colors have been used within each block. Three different sized pinwheels appear within the quilt. Most importantly, the placement of the light and dark elements (which define the design) within the blocks has not always been handled consistently. Therefore, new patterns emerge when one block seemingly joins into another (Figure 7.6).

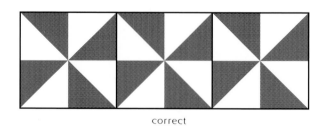

correct

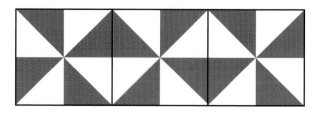

awry

Figure 7.6

BASKETS

✚

Basket patterns are very popular among the Amish. Almost all quilters want to make a baskets quilt at least once in their quilting career. Though baskets are really a type of a repeat block quilt, they'll be handled here as a separate lesson because I feel some further refining is possible.

Once you've selected the baskets pattern you want to work with (Figure 8.1), consider these approaches to handling the color within the individual blocks. (Refer to Lesson 7 for setting suggestions for the completed blocks. Remember the fast method for half-of-a-square triangles in the Appendix.)

 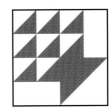 

| Basket | Flower Basket | Indiana Basket |

| Cake Stand | Fruit Basket | Basket |

Figure 8.1

Exercise #1 IDENTICAL COLORATION

Here, the basket units within the quilt must be colored identically. You can use as few as two colors to define the basket design or you may introduce additional colors (Figure 8.2).

A quilt made within these strict limitations still leaves some options. The plain alternate block or lattice can match or contrast with the background. The simplest version would have baskets composed of only two colors with a matching field so that the baskets float. Such a quilt would have an understated elegance (Figure 8.3).

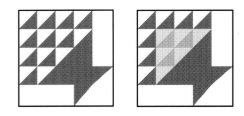

Figure 8.2

Figure 8.3

Exercise #2 ROWS OF COLOR

Another simple format is to work in rows of color. Each row would feature a different color combination for the baskets. Again, these can be made to float by having the same background used for all the baskets and the plain alternate blocks. Or a contrast alternate block can be used as in Photo 11B.

Exercise #3 VARIATION WITHIN THE BLOCK

I particularly encourage you to try this approach, as the average quilter can learn a great deal from this version. Basically, this is a scrap quilt. The blocks will not match each other. Coloration within the blocks isn't limited to two colors as in a Repeat Block quilt. All of the basket quilts pictured in the color photo section are examples of this approach except for Photo 11B. Look carefully.

Photo 12A is the most obvious example of a scrap quilt. Notice that value is handled in such a way that all the baskets aren't clearly defined. Many of them read as different designs even

though all the same pattern pieces are used in each block. One of the reasons this happens in a quilt is that the quilter doesn't understand it is the value difference between the pieces which produces the visual pattern, but instead assumes it is enough to work with different-colored fabrics.

Sometimes fabric fades as a quilt ages. Fabrics which at one time may have had a marked value difference may come to resemble each other more. Not all fabrics age or fade at the same rate, either. Some blocks eventually appear to be made from all the same color. Of course, the quilter won't know this in advance, as it's only visible in a used quilt. It's one aspect that makes an old quilt interesting, however, and you may want to try to emulate this idea.

It is easiest to start with the baskets done as two-fabric blocks. Then play some games. I suggest a glued mock-up in miniature. For example, if you were using the first basket (a four-patch) on page 55, a 3" background square would be a good size with which to work. This time you will cut out the basket pattern parts, so you don't want your sample too small.

I suggest placing the baskets on point. Add a plain block in between to give you more places to add variations in your coloration. Start with one background color, as in the Repeat Block mock-up

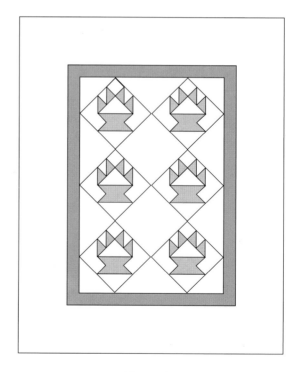

Figure 8.4

(see page 53). Now play with the background in the basket blocks, plain alternate blocks, perimeter and corner triangles (see Figure 8.4 for placement of background shapes). Remember to use colors fairly close together on the color wheel and don't go all the way down to sparkle in your value use. You want the mood to feel like watercolor shading, as if you ran out, and substituted with a similar fabric. Glue on paper when you're satisfied with your background color arrangement.

Determine the color of the baskets by cutting the biggest triangle shape only. Rearrange the choices on the background blocks until you're satisfied with the resulting combinations. You might have a fade-out block, a sparkle block, a block that glows, and a block where a variation is created. Next, cut the smaller triangles, in the same color, needed to finish the pattern; place on the background. Don't glue yet.

Look at each block. Now the fun begins. What can you change? Any part of the basket can be switched to a different version of your original color. Also, parts of the background itself can be changed to something similar. Don't make drastic changes in color or value. Glue when you're pleased with the results.

Audition the inner and outer borders. Glue. If you undertake this approach, you will not be able to make full use of the speedy half-of-a-square triangle method, but the results are worth the extra time it will take you to make the quilt with these variations.

Exercise #4 BACKGROUND PATTERN

It's possible to have a pattern appear in the background blocks. Study Photo 13A. A navy diamond is visible in this quilt. The quilt has been purposely made as a scrap quilt to partially cancel the formality suggested by the diamond. It therefore presents quite an interesting contrast.

CHALLENGE

This lesson groups together four thought-provoking exercises. With these, the planning stage is actually more important than the physical act of sewing. Quilters would benefit from adopting this approach. We often get so involved with the perfection of technique that we don't see the overview. Design and color are what first attract others to our work.

Start with a glued mock-up. Make sure you use a gluestick and not a liquid glue. Remember to place the glue on your white background paper and not on the fabric itself. You'll be making a miniature version of the quilt, so your mock-up won't use much fabric. Sometimes you won't even need to glue the entire quilt in mock-up form. Photo15A is a fragment of Exercise #3. The glued mock-up looked so exciting in this stage that the finished product was constructed as a contemporary Amish quilt.

Exercise #1 CHECKERBOARD

The color wheel can be divided between warm and cool colors (Figure 9.1), each with its warm and its cool side. For example, red with blue in it will feel cooler than red with orange in it. The feeling of temperature is also variable depending on placement within a project. Generally, warm colors come toward you and cool colors recede. Temperature, therefore, presents another method of establishing the feeling of depth in a quilt.

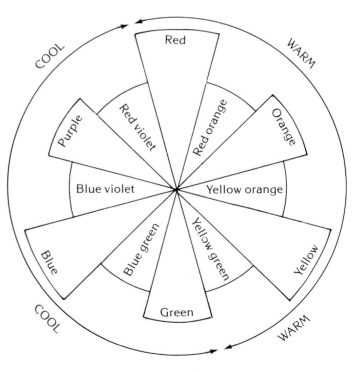

Figure 9.1

Make a Nine-Patch quilt. Use both 5:4 and 4:5 blocks (Lesson 1) in an alternate fashion. If color were not used to differentiate the two kinds of blocks, the quilt would appear as a giant checkerboard, as suggested by Figure 9.2.

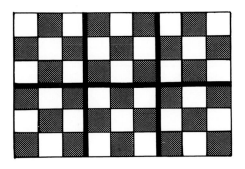

Figure 9.2

Color each 5:4 block with five blacks and four units of a warm color. All 4:5 blocks will have four blacks and five units of a cool color (Figure 9.3).

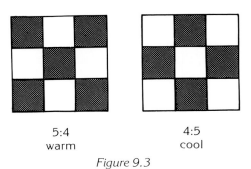

| 5:4 | 4:5 |
| warm | cool |

Figure 9.3

Study Photo 14C; here, a contrasting effect is happening at the same time. The lightest blue nine-patches seem to come toward you, although they should recede because they are cool colors. Also, the darkest red nine-patches, which should come toward you, are actually receding. Value is working to make the light colors advance and the dark ones recede.

Exercise #2 BARN RAISING

Log Cabin quilts have fascinated people for years. Seemingly endless variations can be created by rearranging the individual blocks. A Log Cabin block is half dark and half light, as indicated in Figure 9.4.

In this exercise, you'll get a Log Cabin effect in a Nine-Patch quilt. To accomplish this, the individ-

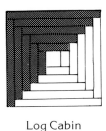

Log Cabin

Figure 9.4

ual nine-patch blocks will have one top corner square and the opposite bottom corner square divided in half. Dark and medium-dark colors will be used for half of the block. Light and medium-light colors will be used for the other side. The center can be of a bright medium if you want it to stand out in the design (Figure 9.5).

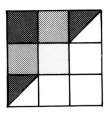

Figure 9.5

Experiment with your colors and values. All the blocks may be handled in an identical fashion, or you may vary the colors within the blocks. Just be consistent in the use of value.

Photo 14A is set in the Barn Raising pattern. The completed blocks are arranged so that the dark sides align to form a visual band. These in turn form a series of concentric diamonds (Figure 9.6).

Exercise #3 INTERIOR ILLUMINATION

Make a quilt which has two basic units: a four-patch and a square-with-two-triangles (Figure 9.7). These two units form a pair. The pairs are then arranged in rows. Sometimes the like units are placed in alternate positions and sometimes the like units are adjacent to each other. The quilt will look like Figure 9.8.

The visual pattern is created by the square-with-two-triangle blocks, provided that one of the trian-

Figure 9.6

Figure 9.8

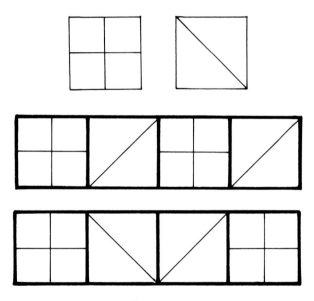

Figure 9.7

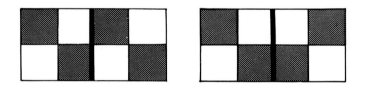

Figure 9.9

gles is of a dark value. These dark triangles link up to create diagonal rows. If you should want part of the rows to disappear, decrease the value difference between the two triangles that form the square.

The four-patches can also create secondary patterns. They can look like a checkerboard or they can blend to create a rectangle (Figure 9.9).

Now you're ready to consider the interior illumination part of this challenge. Through your han-

dling of value you'll be able to control light in this quilt. The Amish quilt on which this exercise is based appears to have a spotlight turned on the center section. This is accomplished by having a lighter "background" in the center area. In Photo 15A the light source seems to be coming from the upper left side of the quilt.

Experiment with the colors of the quilt, with the handling of value, even with whether you want the finished shape to be a square or rectangle. Here is where your glued mock-up will prove invaluable. Photo 15B shows three mock-ups done with varying values

The quilt in Photo 15A is another example of contemporary Amish. The maker ran out of red border fabric and made-do in an Amish fashion. Notice how the quilting beautifully enhances the feeling of a light source.

Exercise #4 CROSS-IN-THE-SQUARE

This time you'll make a scrap Five-Patch quilt set with a lattice. Photo 14B is an example.

The placement of the dark value within each five-patch will establish the visual pattern for that block. There are many possibilities; a few are shown in Figure 9.10.

Once you've made your five-patches, add a lattice with four-patch intersections. (Refer to the Appendix for sewing suggestions.) The lattice should also have a scrap feeling. Position the five-patches on the wall. Audition candidates for the lattice. Work with colors you've already used. Lastly, insert the little connecting four-patches, and add a border to tie everything together.

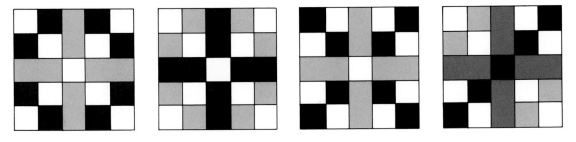

Figure 9.10

OCEAN WAVES

✚

Ocean Waves is both a simple and complex quilt: simple because its main component is the half-of-a-square triangle. (Refer to the Appendix for the fast sewing method.) There are several variations and several ways to set the pattern. The complex part is the handling of color. All sorts of approaches can be taken, so part of the fun will be in making decisions concerning format.

Exercise #1 STANDARD VARIATION

This is the most common way for Ocean Waves to be set. It is visualized as an all-over pattern but can actually be made in rows. Study Photo 16A.

The quilt is composed of "A" and "B" blocks. The placement of the dark value triangle within the half-of-a-square triangle squares is merely reversed in the two kinds of units. The rows of "A" blocks are also staggered with the rows of "B" blocks. This means that the "B" rows will begin and end with half units. Figure 10.1 shows a fragment of such a quilt.

You'll need a total of 240 half-of-a-square triangle units. Depending on the size of these units, you can make the following size quilts (not including borders):

240–1" pieces   = 16" x 24" finished quilt
240–1½" pieces   = 24" x 36" finished quilt
240–2" pieces   = 32" x 48" finished quilt

Figure 10.1

You'll also need 96 individual triangles of the same size as above. These can be added to the grid for the quick sewn half-of-a-square triangles. Draw but don't stitch them when sewing the rest of the grid. See Figure 10.2. Cut. You will get four triangles per square: two of the top color and two of the bottom color. (See Appendix.)

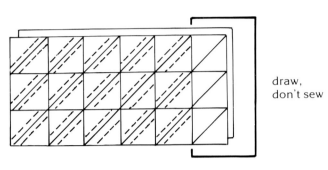

draw, don't sew

Figure 10.2

In addition, you'll need seven large plain squares for the centers of the blocks. To determine the size, multiply four times the finished size of one triangle unit (four units equal the width of a row). Draw a line this length. Bisect it at midpoint with a perpendicular line of the same length. Join the end points to form a square. Add seam allowance. See Figure 10.3. Lastly, you'll need ten large triangles (half of the big squares) to fill in the perimeter.

Work on the wall again. Begin with an "A" row. Place a large square on point. Surround the square

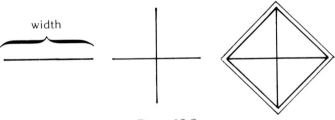

width

Figure 10.3

with small triangles as shown in Figure 10.4. Add half-of-a-square units until you've filled out the block. Check to see that the units are turned in the correct direction.

Next, work on a "B" row. Remember that it will start with one of the large triangles. I find it easiest to begin with a full block which can be plugged in at the midpoint of the "A" row. Then add the two half-blocks needed to fill out the row. See Figure 10.5.

Work across the quilt until all the rows are arranged. Sewing is accomplished by blocks. Study Figures 10.4 and 10.5. There are four sections of triangles and a large square in each block. Complete the triangle sections, then join these, one at a time, to the square. The last seams will be the joining of the triangle units to each other.

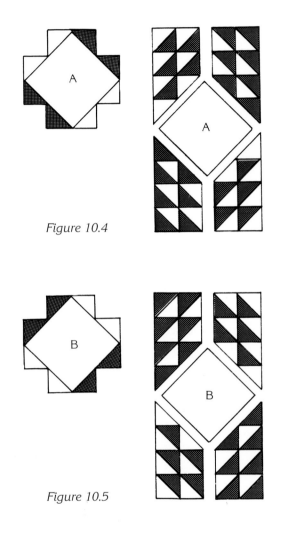

Figure 10.4

Figure 10.5

Now that you understand the approach and techniques involved with the Ocean Waves pattern, it's time to make some color decisions. The quilt may be colored as a scrap quilt, or in diagonal rows of color, or in areas of color.

Making a scrap Ocean Waves is a great challenge. Photo 16A is a pure scrap quilt. The quick triangle method couldn't be employed for this quilt because of the great variety of combinations. You can, however, achieve a scrap appearance and still use the quick method. From your collection, work up the following eight sets:

No. of Set	Value/Value
one	clear light/dark
one	greyed light/dark
one	clear light/medium
two	greyed light/medium
one	medium/medium
two	medium/dark

To test to see if you've come up with a pleasing combination, you can make a glued mock-up. It won't be necessary to make a replica of the whole quilt. Merely make four little models of each set. Arrange them as in Figure 10.6. Cutting out the center blank square will let you audition candidates for that color. You'll need at least two blacks for some of your darks. Without them, there won't be the proper feeling of depth. Notice that only two clear lights are suggested. It's the contrast between the greyed lights and the clear lights that makes the quilt work. When you're pleased with your combination, proceed with the quilt as suggested.

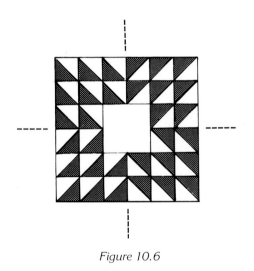

Figure 10.6

Exercise #2 **VARIATION TWO**

The unit of construction will be a nine-patch (Figure 10.7). Four nine-patches are joined for one block. The resulting center square is composed of our triangles. I refer to this variation as a Split Ocean Waves. Figure 10.8 shows four blocks joined. The quilt may be composed of as many of these blocks as desired.

Figure 10.7

Figure 10.8

The basic unit of construction may instead be a four-patch. The resulting quilt will look more complex (Figure 10.9). This quilt lends itself to the idea of working with diagonal rows of color.

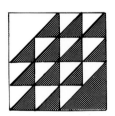

Figure 10.9

Exercise #3 **VARIATION THREE**

This variation is made from nine-patches. Four blocks are joined as in Figure 10.10. Alternate blocks feature dark or light squares in a checkerboard fashion. Diagonal rows will be visible.

The quilt can be made with a minimum of two colors. The result would be very graphic. Don't be afraid to be too simple. Many Ohio and Indiana quilts are made using only two colors.

Figure 10.10

QUILTING

✚

Amish quilters used many of the same motifs that appear in the mainstream of American quilting: feather wreaths, feather plumes, cables, baskets, and flowers. They even had some unique patterns, such as the pumpkin seed. What is unexpected is the coupling of some of these fancy, elaborate designs with the simple lines of the Amish quilt.

This contrast is particularly evident in the Pennsylvania quilts such as the Diamond and the Bars, whose wide borders provide a good canvas for fancy feather designs. The Ohio and Indiana quilts were made from more elaborate pieced repeat designs but, in turn, were more simply quilted. Cables were frequently found in the outer borders.

Why was one quilting design chosen over another? Though some feel that there were religious undertones in the use of the tulip and the rose, I tend to think that availability had a lot to do with it. Some of the pattern use is so widespread that it must have been almost out of habit that the quilters fell back on the same motifs.

Keep the following in mind as you plan your quilting. Amish quilts are flat. To achieve the same look today, use a cotton batt or a piece of flannel. Dark or black thread was used for the quilting stitches. Amish quilters tended to ignore seam lines as a boundary, often superimposing the quilting patterns over an area regardless of individual pieced components. A grid, for example, would run over the whole design field. Or a feather or cable would run all the way around the outer border, even though there would be different color corner blocks. The quilting, therefore, was often like a double exposure image over the pieced pattern of the quilt.

There are several approaches to creating quilting designs. Quilters of today often employ geometric equations and fancy drafting tools. I keep reminding myself that the Amish are a simple people and probably don't know as much math as I do. Many of the patterns used by the Amish can be paper-folded and cut. Let's start with some of the simple images.

Cut paper the size of the space to be filled with quilting. When measuring the area, try not to include seam allowances as it's more difficult to quilt through the additional layers. Work with a large stack of paper so several versions can be cut. Critique your first attempt; then recut. Physically lay the paper pattern on the quilt top to see how it looks. Cutting several variations actually simplifies choosing the most appropriate or best looking. As soon as I cut the first attempt, I can readily see whether it is too fat or too skinny, too flat or too pointed.

A tulip is a good beginning design because most of us have an image in our minds as soon as the word is mentioned. Work with comfortable, sharp scissors. Fold the paper in half and cut. I begin at the top center, but you may begin at the bottom of the design. Remember, the first attempt is merely to get something to critique (Figure 11.1).

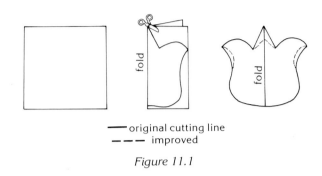

— original cutting line
– – – improved

Figure 11.1

The tulip has many variations and is usually used to fill up a small blank space. It can also be combined with leaves and a vine to create a border, or it can be placed at the end of a feather plume (Figure 11.2).

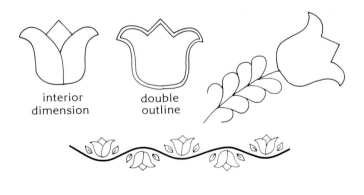

interior dimension   double outline

Figure 11.2

The outline of a basket is another simple, symmetrical shape. Once cut, interior details can be drawn. A series could be used in the wide border

(Figure 11.3). A more complex paper folding will give you some other popular designs. Follow Figure 11.4.

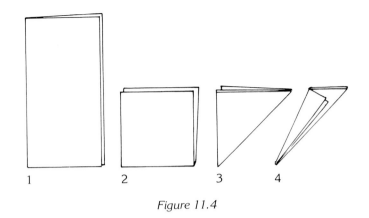

1   2   3   4

Figure 11.4

From this folded shape you can cut an Amish primrose. When appraising the design, figure how many times it is symmetrical. Keep folding until one cut will give you the entire design (Figure 11.5). Traditionally, this design is used in the corner blocks of the narrow inner border. When working with small quilts, you will probably find the space too small to insert this design. However, it would fit nicely in plain alternate blocks between the nine-patches in Lesson 1.

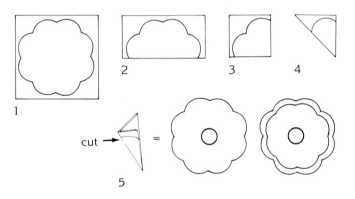

1   2   3   4

cut →   =

5

Figure 11.5

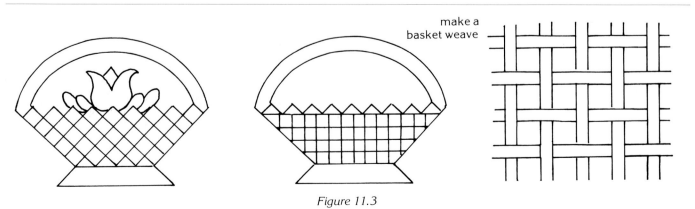

make a basket weave

Figure 11.3

From this shape, you can also make an eight-pointed star. When you make the fourth fold, a triangle of paper extends beyond the main body. Fold this down, and then cut parallel to this edge. See Figure 11.6. This star is traditionally found in the center of an Amish Diamond. It is filled with concentric smaller stars. Or it can be used as a fill-in design (Figure 11.7).

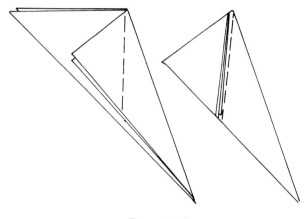

Figure 11.6

A cable is another paper-folding design. Cut a rectangle of paper equal to the length and width of the desired cable. If the cable is for a large quilt, the paper can represent one section of the area, such as one-half or one-third of the length. Keep folding this in half until you have a suitable size for one link of cable. (If you prefer an odd number of lengths in your cable, refer to the Appendix for help in dividing a space into a given number of divisions.) Fold this shape in half twice and cut as shown in Figure 11.8. Now, draw in the connecting lines and you'll have a custom-sized cable.

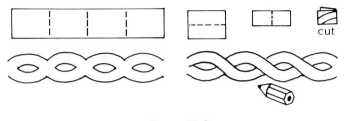

Figure 11.8

To make a cable go around a corner, cut a piece of paper the size of the corner. Diagonally fold it in half. Whatever happens on one half will automatically be duplicated on the other side. Therefore, make sure that your cable ends at the same place in the design on both sides of the corner. See Figure 11.9. Feather plumes are another common border design. In essence, the design is a vine with attached paisley shapes. Figure out where you want the vine to go and then add the paisleys. Paper-folding can be employed to determine the contour limits of the vine by controlling both the

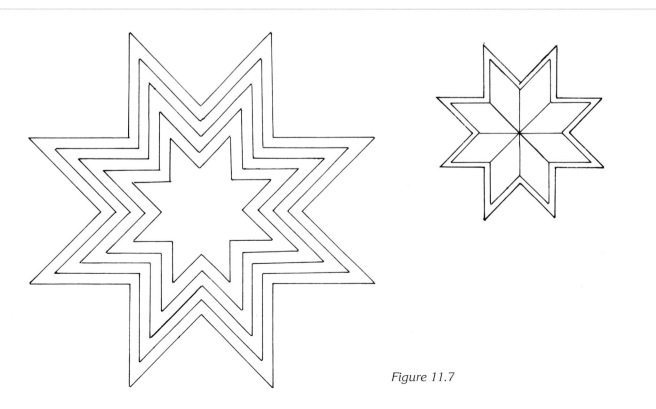

Figure 11.7

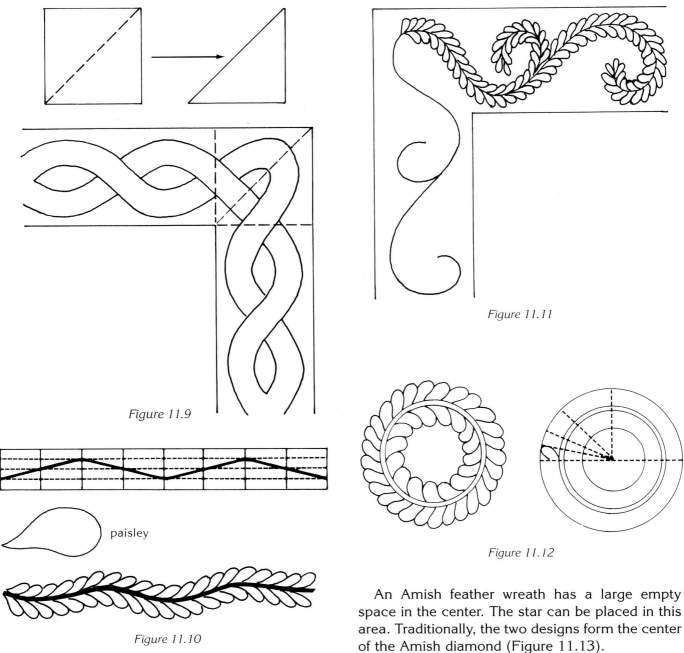

Figure 11.11

Figure 11.9

paisley

Figure 11.10

Figure 11.12

An Amish feather wreath has a large empty space in the center. The star can be placed in this area. Traditionally, the two designs form the center of the Amish diamond (Figure 11.13).

width of the curve and the frequency of the ups and downs. See Figure 11.10.

The Amish have many variations on the feather plume. There are often appendages branching off the main vine. See Figure 11.11. When the feather is turned into a circular motif, it's called a wreath. The Quaker feather wreath is common throughout the quilt world. Three concentric circles control the perimeters of the wreath and establish the central vine. Paper-fold the circle to determine a good size for the paisley pattern (Figure 11.12).

Figure 11.13

A grapevine can be used as a border or within a design, such as in a Bars quilt. Establish the placement of the vine, as for the feather plume, then add the grapes and leaves. See Figure 11.14.

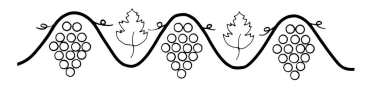

Figure 11.14

A rose is another popular plant form. Roses are used to fill up spaces, such as the large triangles in a Diamond. The flower doesn't lend itself to paper cutting, but it can easily be drawn. Follow Figure 11.15.

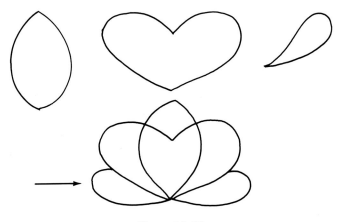

Figure 11.15

The pumpkin seed design is traditionally placed in the narrow inner border. It won't fit on a small quilt, but sometimes fragments of the design can be adapted for alternate plain blocks or in borders (Figure 11.16).

1. draw the square on point
2. add 3 parallel lines
3. add pumpkin seed—do like a figure-eight

Figure 11.16

Another wonderful linear shape is made from interlocking half circles. Photo 12A shows the shape used in conjunction with a grid and in the narrow

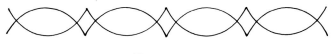

Figure 11.17

inner border. See also Figure 11.17. Overlapping circles, sometimes called fans, make a nice, simple border design (Figure 11.18).

The use of grids is widespread in Amish quilts, particularly in the Ohio and Indiana versions. The grid can be used as a background, as in Photo 11A. More importantly, a grid can be laid over the central design area as in Photo 9A. Grids are frequently used as a border, as in Photos 13A and 16B. The simplest solution would be to superimpose a grid over the whole quilt as in Photos 8A and 9B.

Figure 11.18

Grids can be easily marked with masking tape directly onto the quilt top while you're quilting. Use a ruler as a straightedge. Masking tape comes in various widths, even as narrow as ¼"; check your local quilt or paint store. Mark only one line at a time and don't keep the tape on overnight. Figure 11.19 shows some of the common grids. Study the photos closely for examples of contemporary solutions to quilting. Don't be afraid to try your own new version of a design.

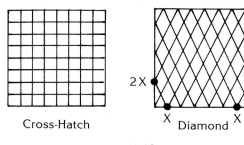

Diagonal   Double Diagonal   Triple Diagonal

Cross-Hatch   Diamond

Figure 11.19

APPENDIX

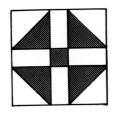

I. Drafting

  A. Nomenclature (Pieced quilt block patterns can be placed into categories to simplify their drafting and construction.)

    1. Nine-patch: divisible by three (Figure 12.1).

Figure 12.1

    2. Four-patch: divisible by four (Figure 12.2).

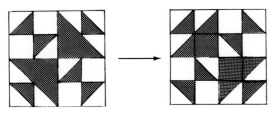

Figure 12.2

    3. Five-patch: divisible by five (Figure 12.3).
    4. Seven-patch: divisible by seven (Figure 12.4).

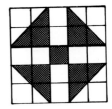

Figure 12.3

Figure 12.4

  B. Drafting Procedure

    1. Identify category.
    2. Draw square desired (finished size).
    3. Divide square into proper grid.
    4. Fill in pattern.
    5. Identify individual shapes.
    6. Add seam allowance to pattern shapes (Figure 12.5).

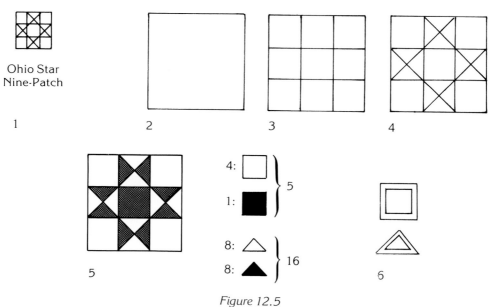

Ohio Star
Nine-Patch

1   2   3   4

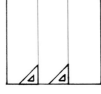

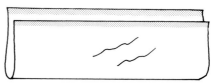

4: ⬜ }
1: ⬛ } 5

8: △ }
8: ▲ } 16

5   6

Figure 12.5

C. Division of space into given number of equal units
1. Draw square desired size
2. Identify next measurement past square size that is divisible by grid number.
3. Position ruler so that one end touches the bottom left-hand corner; swing ruler up right-hand side until measurement from #2 is reached.
4. Divide measurement from #2 by grid number; make marks at these intervals along ruler.
5. Use a right angle to draw lines.
6. Repeat procedure for division lines going in second direction (Figure 12.6).

Quick Piecing
A. Strip Piecing
1. Preparation of fabric: prewash; remove from dryer before over-dried. Fold in half, selvage to selvage. Realign until fabric hangs straight, which indicates it is on grain (Figure 12.7).

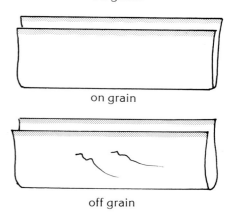

off grain.

on grain

off grain

Figure 12.7

2. Fold fabric lengthwise once again. Use a right angle to true-up one end. Pin to hold in place (Figure 12.8).

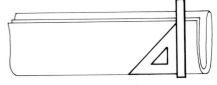

Figure 12.8

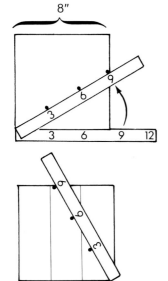

8"

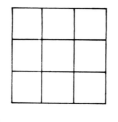

Figure 12.6

3. Cut into widths of desired measurement, using rotary cutter or scissors that will cut through four layers. Each strip will be equal to width of fabric.

4. Join two strips by machine. Press seam allowance in one direction. Join additional strips as required; sew each time in the opposite direction to keep the unit from curving. Press after each addition (Figure 12.9).

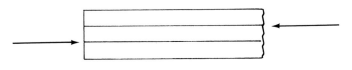

Figure 12.9

5. Construct strips of proper configuration to make desired units (Figure 12.10).

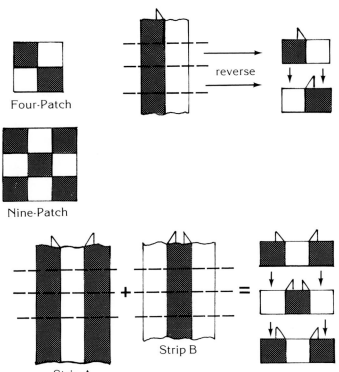

Figure 12.10

6. When joining prefabbed units, match at seam intersections. With advance planning, the seam allowances will be pressed in opposite directions. With practice, you can eliminate the need to pin. Merely couple the units together at the correct juncture. The opposing seam allowances help. The time spent practicing is worthwhile because of the time ultimately saved (Figure 12.11).

Figure 12.11

B. Half-of-a-Square Triangles (Thanks to Barbara Johannah for this colossal idea.)

1. Determine desired size of finished triangle unit. To this always add ⅞" to determine X (Figure 12.12).

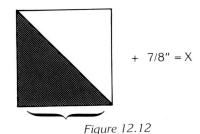

+ 7/8" = X

Figure 12.12

2. Draw a grid on the wrong side of one of the fabrics to be used for the triangle units. The grid should contain enough squares to equal half the number of completed units desired (Figure 12.13).

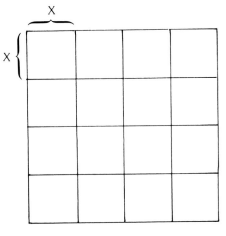

Figure 12.13

3. Draw diagonal lines across the grid (Figure 12.14).

4. Add ¼" seam allowance lines (Figure 12.15).

5. Position fabric with grid over second fabric to be used for triangle units, right sides together. Pin. Sew along seam allowance lines, up one

seam and down the next. Skip across un-marked corners (Figure 12.16).

6. Press and cut. Press individual units (Figure 12.17).

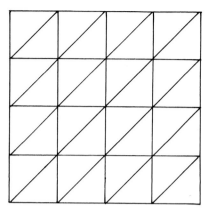

Figure 12.14

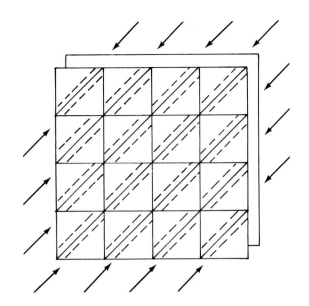

Figure 12.16

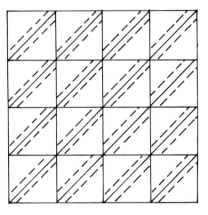

Figure 12.15

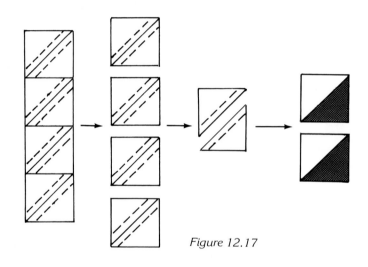

Figure 12.17

III. Construction of Quilt Top

A. True-up Blocks

1. Measure width and height of all blocks.
2. Determine smallest size. Make a square this measurement to be used as a master pattern.
3. Using the master pattern, trim all blocks. Blocks must agree to within ⅛" (Figure 12.18).

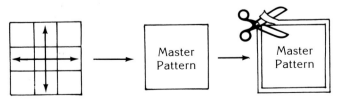

Figure 12.18

B. Perimeter Triangles (Figure 12.19).

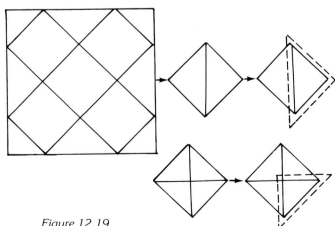

Figure 12.19

C. Joining Rows (Figure 12.20).

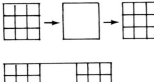

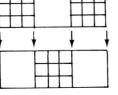

Figure 12.20

D. Lattice (Figure 12.21).

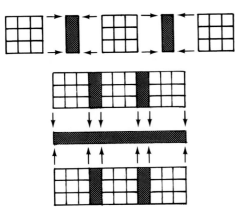

Figure 12.21

E. Borders (Figure 12.22).

F. Binding (final step after quilting)
1. Cut strips on grain 2" wide; fold in half length-wise and press.
2. Pin to front of quilt, on opposite edges. Trim even with quilt edge, and sew (Figure 12.23).

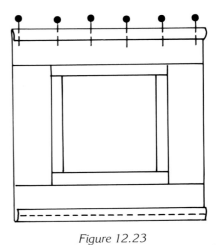

Figure 12.23

3. Pin to remaining two edges; overhanging ½" at ends. Sew. Fold to back side; tuck in over-hangs. Hem by hand (Figure 12.24).

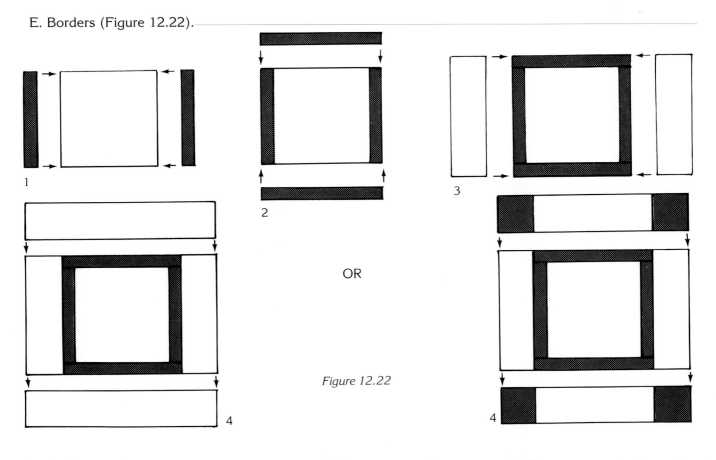

OR

Figure 12.22

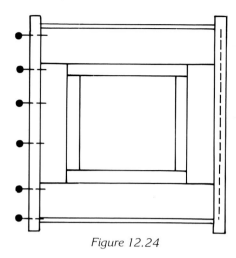

Figure 12.24

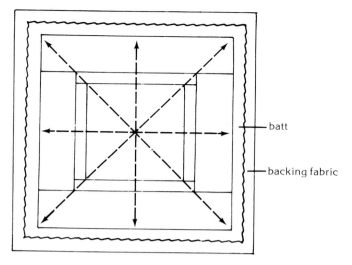

Figure 12.25

4. If the quilt is to be used as a wallhanging, a rod pocket can be sewn to the quilt back at the same time. Position a strip of desired width on back, along edge, right side up. Stitch through binding, quilt, and rod pocket. Turn under seam allowance on remaining edge; stitch by hand.

IV. Quilting
A. Basting (Figure 12.25).
B. Quilting stitch (Figure 12.26).

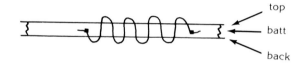

Figure 12.26

BIBLIOGRAPHY

✚

BOOKS ABOUT AMISH QUILTS:

Bishop, Robert. *New Discoveries in American Quilts.* New York: Dutton, 1975.

Bishop, Robert and Safanda, Elizabeth. *A Gallery of Amish Quilts.* New York: Dutton, 1976.

Granih, Eve Wheatcroft. *The Amish Quilt.* Intercourse, Pennsylvania: Good Books, 1989.

Haders, Phyllis. *Sunshine and Shadow, The Amish and Their Quilts.* New York: Universe Books, 1976.

Hughes, Robert and Silber, Julie. *Amish: The Art of the Quilt.* New York: Alfred A. Knopf, 1990.

Pellman, Rachel and Kenneth. *A Treasury of Amish Quilts.* Intercourse, Pennsylvania: Good Books, 1990.

Pellman, Rachel and Kenneth. *Amish Crib Quilts.* Intercourse, Pennsylvania: Good Books, 1985.

Pellman, Rachel and Kenneth. *The World of Amish Quilts.* Intercourse, Pennsylvania: Good Books, 1984.

Pottinger, David. *Quilts from the Indiana Amish, A Regional Collection.* New York: Dutton, 1983.

Woodward, Thomas and Greenstein, Blanche. *Crib Quilts and Other Small Wonders.* New York: Dutton, 1981.

BOOKS ABOUT THE AMISH WAY OF LIFE:

Bender, Sue. *Plain and Simple: A Woman's Journey to the Amish.* San Francisco: Harper & Row Publishers, 1989.

Coleman, Bill. *Amish Odyssey.* New York: Van Der Marck Editions, 1988.

Cragg, Perry. *The Amish, A Photographic Album.* Cleveland, Ohio: Dillon/Liederbach, 1971.

Good, Merle. *Who Are the Amish?* Intercourse, Pennsylvania: Good Books, 1985.

Hostetler, John A. *The Amish.* Scottdale, Pennsylvania: Herald Press, 1982.

Hostetler, John A. *Amish Life.* Scottdale, Pennsylvania: Herald Press, 1981.

Hostetler, John A. *Amish Roots: A Treasury of History, Wisdom, and Lore.* Baltimore, Maryland: The Johns Hopkins University Press, 1989.

Hostetler, John A. *Amish Society.* Baltimore, Maryland: Johns Hopkins University Press, 1980.

McCauley, Daniel and Kathryn. *Decorative Arts of the Amish of Lancaster County.* Intercourse, Pennsylvania: Good Books, 1988.

Scott, Stephen. *Plain Buggies.* Lancaster, Pennsylvania: Good Books, 1981.

Seitz, Ruth Hoover. *Amish Country.* New York: Crescent Books, 1987.

Seitz, Ruth Hoover. *Amish Ways.* Harrisburg, Pennsylvania: RB Books, 1991.

Zielinski, John M. *The Amish: A Pioneer Heritage.* Des Moines, Iowa: Wallace-Homestead Book Co., 1975.

Zielinski, John M. *The Amish Across America.* Grinnell, Iowa: Iowa Heritage Galleries, 1983.

ABOUT THE AUTHOR

Roberta Horton of Berkeley, California, has been a quiltmaker since 1970. She is the author of five quiltmaking books and has taught and lectured worldwide. She is known for her flair with color, which she attributes to her study of Amish quilts. Fascination with the Amish lifestyle, which she feels is expressed in their quilts, has made her seek simplicity in her own work.